Create You Electronic Office

Mark Neely

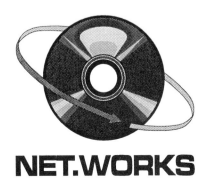

NET.WORKS

NET.WORKS

Net.Works, PO Box 200

Harrogate, N.Yorks

HG1 2YR   England

Email: sales@net-works.co.uk

UK Fax: 01423-526035

Net.Works is an imprint of Take That Ltd.

Published in association with Maximedia Pty Ltd
PO Box 529Kiama, NSW 2533, Australia.

ISBN: 1 873668 44 9
Design © 1997 Take That Ltd.
Text ©1997 Infolution Pty Ltd.
Cartoons ©1997 Maximedia Pty Ltd

10 9 8 7 6 5 4 3 2 1

Trademarks:
Trademarked names are used throughout this book. Rather than place a trademark symbol in every occurance of a trademark name, the names are being used only in an editorial fashion for the benefit of the trademark owner, with no intention to infringe the trademark.

Printed and bound in The United Kingdom

Disclaimer:
The information in this book is distributed on an "as is" basis, without warranty. While very effort has been made to ensure that this book is free from errors or omissions, neither the author, the publisher, or their respective employees and agents, shall have any liability to any person or entity with respect to any liability, loss or damage caused or alleged to have been caused directly or indirectly by advice or instructions contained in this book or by the computer hardware or software products described herein. **Readers are urged to seek prior expert advice before making decisions, or refraining from making decisions, based on information or advice contained in this book.**

Contents

Preface.. 5

Working for Yourself 6

Getting Started 12

1. The Small Business Advantage 19

2. Your Home Office 23

3. Your Telephone System 28

4. ISDN Technology 37

5. Mobile Phones 40

6. Answering Machines 50

7. Using a Pager and Voicemail 53

8. Buying a Fax Machine 57

9. Buying a Personal Organiser 61

10. Buying an Office PC 66

11. Buying a Printer 74

12. Buying a Scanner 79

13. Harnessing the Internet 82

14. Difficulties Facing the Mobile Office 86

15. Time Management 89

Appendix: Your Business Plan 92

Special Reader Offer
Business Shareware & Freeware

Here's your chance to acquire a great business software library to evaluate on your own computer. The programs listed below are Shareware, which means you can evaluate them in your own time — and only pay a registration fee to the author if and when you decide to use the program regularly. Save time — and cut down on costs — with your computer!

Note: In most cases software which requires Windows 3.x will also run under Windows 95. Programs specifically designed for Windows 95 however will not run under Windows 3.x.

DISK 1- Account Pro for Windows

Easy full-featured double-entry accounting program. Handles up to 2000 books, with 1000 accounts and 16,300 transactions each. The system includes budgeting, and handles custom-accounting periods. A manual in WRI format also includes information on double-entry bookkeeping. System Requirements: 4MB RAM, Visual Basic 3.0 runtime module (incl.), and Windows 3.1x.

DISK2- DayWatch

Complete time-management utility suite. Track your daily activities, appointments, projects, and more. The program includes an event list manager, full-screen project calendar, daily journal with user-defined data fields, date calculator, forecast window, find and categorize functions, data sharing, font selection, and sound and picture attachments. System Requirements: Modem, Visual Basic 3.0 runtime module, and Windows 3.x.

Chartist

Easy business graphics flowcharting package for Windows. Just drag and drop from the program's symbol library to create a variety of flow and organisational charts. Shapes are easily connected using Chartist's autorouting lines, which are available in several styles. Full color and font support and can export documents through the Clipboard in either .wmf or ...bmp format. It also offers support for its own brand of hypertext jumps, linked to symbols. System Requirements: Windows 3.1x.

DISK3 - Yeah Write

Written by former employees of WordPerfect, this is a 32-bit word processor which uses colorful, easy-to-read tabbed screens that resemble loose-leaf notebook paper. Instead of starting each document with a lot of formatting decisions, Yeah Write lets you fill in the blanks of predefined docu-

ments. You can import and export WordPerfect 5.1 documents and use spell checking and fonts. Upon registration, you get access to an address book, Internet FTP Save and Retrieve, envelope support, email and faxing features, and more. Although Yeah Write is a shareware program, you can use this unregistered version for as long as you like. The 'free' edition, which contains about 70% of the features of the licensed version, includes diary, general-purpose, journal, business letter, personal letter, memo, and notes documents. System Requirements: Windows 95.

DISK 4 - Small Business Inventory Control

Easy-to-use inventory program designed for small businesses. It lets you track vendor information, such as name, ID, contact names, addresses, and phone and fax numbers, for both primary and secondary vendors. Quickly get a handle on your inventory by entering name, number, vendor, description, reorder levels and quantities, quantity stock, item cost, and selling price. You can search, sort, or perform queries on your inventory items; maintain customer lists; track items sold; and order and receive items. Two reports are available: Individual Item Report and a Whole Inventory Report. System Requirements: Windows 95.

DISK 5 - VistaCalc

Inexpensive alternative to commercial spreadsheets. Provides an extensive array of math and financial functions as well as some powerful graphing features. The help is detailed and well organized, making VistaCalc an excellent introduction tool for someone who wants to learn spreadsheet operations without a big investment. System Requirements: Windows 3.1x.

Continued on page 49 ⇨

Preface

Leaving a big corporate office - and regular pay cheques - to start your own small business opens the door to potential prosperity. It also offers many challenges.

I discovered this when, several years ago, I left a large private law firm to start a home-based information technology and Internet consulting business. Although working for myself has proved more satisfying than I ever imagined, I have learned many lessons along the way - especially regarding the technological needs of a small or home office.

I have spent considerable time over the last few years helping other small and home-based businesses come to terms with their computing and office equipment needs.

Too often I have met people who attempted to establish or upgrade a small office/home office (SOHO) without assistance, making embarrassing and costly mistakes. A common cause of problems is the absence of a detailed or considered technology plan. Failing to properly integrate information technology can have disastrous effects on any business, large or small.

Within the last decade or so, SOHOs have gradually adopted technology traditionally associated with larger offices, such as "intelligent" telephones, facsimile machines, photocopiers and more. Not coincidentally, over the same period attitudes towards small businesses and home offices have changed dramatically. No longer considered the "country cousins" of big business, SOHOs now compete aggressively and successfully with larger companies, making good use of the flexibility their business structure allows.

Larger companies have recently shown an interest in harnessing the benefits which can flow from allowing employees to telecommute; that is, work away from the office (either on the road or from their own home or office).

This book aims to explore the different types of technology that a home-based worker requires to be productive and to compete within the modern business environment. Regardless of whether you are operating a part-time business, a SOHO or telecommuting, you will find the guidance you need inside.

Despite this obvious technology bias, you will also find valuable tips and insights to help decide whether working from home is for you, and how to go about realising your dream!

Mark Neely

Introduction

Working for Yourself

If you have browsed through the computer or business section of your local bookstore or library lately, you will have noticed the proliferation of books and magazines which predict the coming of a new era. The *"electronic office"* revolution, they tell us, is set to reform the traditional business model of a centralised workforce and multi-tiered management.

Gradually, business is moving from the entrenched office management structure of the Industrial Age, toward smaller, self-managing Information Age units.

Futurists and management advisors predict a further "flattening" of the management structure, as companies confront the increasing speed of events in the modern business world by bringing decision makers closer to the front line.

This paradigm shift in corporate structures isn't only of concern to owners and corporate theorists. Workers, both at management and shop-floor levels, have been following this vision of the future with interest.

Corporate managers, always keen to keep their workforce lean and the bottom line healthy, are examining the causes and results of this shift in the contemporary business model.

Studies have shown that allowing employees to telecommute from home (or even decentralised offices) has a positive effect on both staff morale and productivity.

Some managers have also realised that by "empowering" workers and allowing them to work from home or some other non-central location, office space requirements and associated overheads can be reduced.

But perhaps the biggest beneficiaries of this paradigm shift are owners of small businesses and the self-employed.

Small businesses and individuals are embracing this decentralised business model, and moving to the suburbs to escape the costs associated with prime central business district (CBD) locations.

This new breed of small business, operating from homes and small offices in typically residential areas, is gaining increasing legitimacy. So much so that the acronym SOHO - Small Office/Home Office - has been coined to describe it.

In addition, they have been recognised by government and business agencies for their substantial contribution to the economy and to employment figures.

The move to "decentralise" the CBD has allowed individuals who previously may not have been able to afford to lease and furnish business premises the option of establishing legitimate home-based businesses.

This offers an exciting career path for budding entrepreneurs yet to enter the workforce, workers who are looking for a new challenge, and those people who have always dreamed of working for themselves.

Why work from home?

Working from home offers many benefits, both personal and financial. These advantages include:

Family considerations

The prime motivation for many home-based workers is to be closer to their families.

These workers are able to spend more time with their spouses and watch their children grow up.

They reject the notion that the breadwinner must slave away at a distant office, often leaving for work before the children rise, and returning home after they are asleep. Working from home allows parents to play a larger role in their children's lives, without having to sacrifice income or skills development.

Working from home also offers potential savings on child minding and related expenses. Having one or both spouses working from home brings greater flexibility in meeting child-minding needs.

Be your own boss

Many home-based workers are attracted to the thought of being their own boss.

Working for yourself can be invigorating, and provide a sense of true financial independence. It also requires - as many people discover within the first months - a great deal of focus and self-discipline. We will look at these issues in the following chapters.

Flexibility is another motivating factor. Balancing a finite number of hours between work, family, social responsibilities, recreation and hobbies becomes much easier when you can choose your working hours - especially once you have reclaimed the time wasted commuting to and from an office.

Variation in office hours

Some people find it difficult to work a traditional nine-to-five shift.

Creative people are often at their most productive late at night or in the early mornings, and find it hard to capture that energy during the set working hours demanded by office life.

Equally, working from home enables workaholics to plough on through the weekends - and even remain productive when they are sick.

Freedom to roam

Workers in many industries and professions, such as sales, can find that being tied to an office limits their ability to liaise with and service clients.

Workers who telecommute remain in contact with the office while on the road, allowing them to be far more productive and responsive to client needs.

Special needs

Working from home provides the physically challenged with more control over their working environment, as a home office can more easily be modified to cater for specific needs.

Society benefits, too!

An increase in the number of home-based and decentralised office workers benefits both the individuals and companies involved, and the community.

Home-based workers do not - by definition - need to commute to work each morning, thus reducing the number of cars using highways and roads. As telecommuting and home-based businesses become more mainstream, traffic congestion will decrease, as will much traffic-generated pollution.

Workers who commute to a decentralised office are also more likely to avoid main arterial roads, which will lead to reduced congestion and traffic snarls. These modifications to our society's driving patterns may even decrease the frustration drivers experience when caught in traffic, reducing the incidence of "road rage" and similar anti-social activities.

Is a SOHO for everyone?

Despite the benefits a SOHO offers, working from home does not suit everyone.

Household distractions - TV, children, neighbours and the like - can be too overwhelming for some people. In addition, some workers are unable to adjust to the increased time they spend with their spouses.

Previously office-bound workers may miss the "camaraderie" and office chit-chat to which they have grown accustomed. Although some home-based workers relish the lack of office distractions and the associated boost in productivity, many workers miss the regular interruptions from co-workers, finding the isolation disconcerting.

Some telecommuters fear that being "out of sight" will truly lead to being "out of mind" - with disastrous effects on their career prospects.

In addition, working from home won't suit some workers, such as those who require daily meetings with clients. A home-office may be impractical, unless arrangements can be made to meet with clients at a convenient location.

This book

This book introduces readers to the issues involved in setting up an office, either as a place from which to run a business, or as a home-base for telecommuters and mobile workers.

It canvasses all aspects of outfitting a SOHO, ranging from choosing the right computer and mobile telephone, to the office space itself. Advanced topics (such as using email, voice mail and videoconferencing to keep in contact with clients and the office) are also addressed.

Most home offices are occupied by those starting a new business. Therefore, the first section of this book is devoted to issues involved in starting your own business.

The remaining chapters discuss the technological aspects of equipping a SOHO, offering advice for both novices and experienced users of technology.

→ Chapter 1 helps you answer the question "Why do I want to be my own boss?", examining financial and quality-of-life issues that motivate self-employed individuals.

→ In Chapter 2, we discuss the advantages offered by small or home-based businesses.

→ Chapter 3 outlines the process involved in establishing a home-office, including tips to help you avoid common home-office mistakes.

→ Chapter 4 provides comprehensive advice on selecting a new telephone system, as well as some handy tips on how to save money in the process.

→ Chapter 5 discusses the comparatively new ISDN technology, which can significantly increase the efficiency of technology - at a price.

→ Mobile phones - fast becoming a business necessity - are canvassed in Chapter 6, which lists important features to look for when choosing a mobile phone.

→ If you work by yourself, messaging technology, such as answering machines and voice and paging services, can be a boon. These are discussed in Chapters 7 and 8 respectively.

→ Although facsimile machines have become cheaper in recent years, there are still a number of issues you should be aware of before buying one. Chapter 9 highlights these.

→ Personal organisers - the handiest of business gadgets - are discussed in Chapter 10.

→ The essential tools of a modern office, PCs and notebook computers, are dealt with in Chapters 11 and 12.

→ Choosing the best printer and scanner to meet your needs is canvassed in Chapters 13 and 14, while Chapter 15 introduces you to the emerging all-in-one office devices.

→ In Chapter 16 we take a look at the Internet, and how many businesses around the globe are benefiting from an Internet connection.

➜ Desktop videoconferencing, the 90s alternative to time-consuming (and expensive) business trips, is addressed in Chapter 17.

➜ In Chapter 18 we highlight difficulties that confront the "mobile" computer user, especially those who travel overseas.

➜ And, finally, in Chapter 19 we offer advice on time management, one of the most important skills a self-employed worker can possess.

➜ Appendix I will help those establishing a new venture to develop a business plan to show to potential investors or financiers.

Contacting me

I always welcome feedback from my readers (positive or otherwise). You can contact me via my publisher's office at:

Mark Neely

c/o Take That Ltd.

PO Box 200

Harrogate

HG1 2YR

or by emailing me direct at:

mpn@bigpond.com

Chapter 1

Getting Started

Starting your own small business is perhaps best likened to a game of chess. If you make a mistake - no matter how small - in the opening moves, you may suffer difficulties at a later stage. It might even cost you the game.

Statistics show approximately one in every three new small business ventures fail. The best way to increase your chance of success is to map out every detail of your business venture - **before** committing your money. Careful planning will help you to become aware of many aspects of the business you might not otherwise consider.

The key to planning is the development of a detailed, written business plan. As well as increasing your awareness of all aspects of the business, this plan will be valuable when you apply for finance, and during progress reviews.

We look at the process of creating a business plan in the Appendix.

Your Own Business

The first question to ask yourself when considering whether to start a home-based business is "Why?". What are your motivations for working for yourself?

Be your own boss

The desire to be your own boss may be your main motivation. The idea of managing a business is very alluring indeed!

Financial independence

Many people want to ensure their financial security. Working for yourself puts you in control of your finances, and ensures you are aware of all the financial issues that affect you. Self-employed workers also have a certain amount of freedom in determining their income and devising a tax-efficient salary package.

Leveraging your skills

Do you possess certain skills that are currently in demand? Is your employer utilising them, and are you receiving adequate remuneration? If not, consider setting yourself up as a consultant or independent contractor, earning a much higher income than before.

Creative freedom

Do you yearn to have greater control over the way in which your skills and abilities are utilised? Being self-employed puts you in control of the type of work you do and for whom you work.

Flexible working hours

Would you like to decide the number of hours you work, and when you work these?

More time with your family

Working for yourself, especially from home, gives you more scope for spending quality time with your spouse and family.

What Business?

The type of business you start depends on a number of factors. Many of these are personal, but there are a few practical issues as well.

TIP

Beware trend information. Many people considering starting a new business ask: What was successful last year? Recent success stories can provide insight into the type of business which will be successful in the future. However, be wary of placing too much emphasis on past success.

Personal considerations

Starting a small business from scratch is not for everyone. It often entails a lot of hard work, a long working week, and many sacrifices.

It is wise, therefore, to consider businesses which reflect your interests. If you enjoy your work, your prospects of long-term success will naturally increase.

To determine which type of business is "right" for you, ask yourself the following questions:

❑   What skills (personal, technical, managerial and professional) have I developed that are currently in demand (or may be in demand in the near future)?

    Be honest in your assessment, and solicit the opinions of friends, family, colleagues and past employers.

❑   How do I spend my spare/recreational time? Do I have any hobbies that could be transformed into a business?

    For instance, if you are a dab hand at woodwork or pottery, you might establish a craft shop, or make children's toys.

❑   Do I have time to run a business?

    Not everyone quits his or her day job to start a business. Many people choose to establish a part-time business by working after-hours and on weekends. This allows them to gauge the success of their venture before leaving the "safety net" of employment.

❑   Do I have my family's support?

    Starting a new business can be both exciting and stressful. Being able to count on the support of those around you is an enormous help.

Practical considerations

There are, similarly, a number of practical considerations.

For instance, how much money do you have saved or available to start a new venture? Obviously, those people on a limited budget have fewer choices than those with substantial financial backing.

Explore your potential marketplace before deciding on a business. After all, only a foolish person would open a fashion boutique in a nudist colony!

Try to ascertain the goods and services your neighbourhood needs, but which are not currently available or are inconvenient to access (in terms of travelling distance or the way in which they are offered).

For example, in a neighbourhood comprised predominantly of young working parents, there may be a strong demand for child-care services or domestic help. If you live in a rural area, there might be a demand for your carpentry skills.

Pair your business idea with the needs of people who live nearby, as they are likely to be your initial customers!

Filling a Niche

It follows, therefore, that the smoothest path to a successful business is to find a niche in the marketplace that matches your skills.

To determine whether your proposed business venture fills such a niche, ask yourself:

- ☐ What type of business would I like to start? What would be its primary focus? Will it also have a secondary focus?
- ☐ What products/services will I sell?
- ☐ Who would be my competition?
- ☐ Who will be my customers? Do they live nearby?

The Competition

It is rare to conceive a business that is completely unique and without competition. Therefore, it is imperative to assess your competition:

- ☐ How long have they been in business?
- ☐ What is their business model (that is, how do they operate)?
- ☐ What are their strengths and weaknesses? For instance, do they have an excellent reputation with a loyal client base?
- ☐ How can I compete?

> **TIP**
>
> *Look closely at your pricing structure. The price at which you offer your products or services should cover both your fixed costs (such as equipment and supplies, rent and wages) and variable costs (such as marketing and promotional expenses), as well as provide the desired profit margin.*

Very few newcomers can successfully compete with an established competitor. That is, unless they discover and exploit its weaknesses.

For example, John Richardson is a brilliant programmer who can see a market for an office automation program he has designed. However, a competitor who has been operating for a number of years has over half the potential market sewn up.

John realises that he cannot compete with the rival company in terms of marketing clout, toll-free support services or fancy manuals. But he has heard users of the rival product complain that it lacks several refinements, such as a user-friendly interface, help menus and so on.

Seeing a chance to distinguish his product, and compete with the opposition on a winnable issue, John incorporates these ideas into his software and makes several profitable sales within weeks.

The moral? In a market crowded with competitors, it is important to differentiate your product or service.

The standard tactic adopted by newcomers is to offer the product or service more cheaply. Unless you can offer comparable services with lower overheads, this is not a wise move, as it can seriously affect your long-term profitability.

A better alternative is to distinguish your business in terms of quality, service or greater flexibility (this can relate to features offered by your product or the way in which you provide services).

Further Issues

Having analysed the personal and practical considerations of starting a business, the type of business which best suits your skills, interests and lifestyle, and the niche market opportunities and competition in your area, you may think that you are ready to begin.

Not so fast!

There are still several important issues to address. Some you can confidently undertake yourself. In the case of others, you will need to seek advice, either from your local Office of Business Affairs or from a professional advisor.

It pays to be cautious and ensure that you understand each issue, and its possible repercussions.

What will my legal structure be?

Most home-based businesses operate as "sole traders"; that is, as individuals with no specific legal arrangements. This means that the business trades as a private individual, without any clear distinction between company and personal assets.

TIP

Avoid overspending on overheads, such as rent and equipment, especially when there is some risk that the venture may not succeed. If you cannot work from home, take out a short-term lease on premises and negotiate a 'buy-back' clause into your equipment purchase contract or leasing agreement. Set yourself a series of goals which, when achieved, will indicate that your business has a healthy future, and tie purchasing decisions to these.

However, it might be more advantageous to incorporate a company or, if more than one person is involved, establish a partnership. It is always advisable to seek professional advice from your lawyer or accountant in this regard.

Do I need a licence to operate?

Depending on the nature of your business, you might require one or a number of licences from several different government departments. Talk to your lawyer, or contact your local DTI office for details.

Do I need insurance?

Most businesses require public liability insurance, in the event that someone is injured as a result of using their products or services. If you are investing in office equipment, also insure against theft, fire and other contingencies.

Are zoning issues involved?

Some local councils prohibit the establishment of home offices which involve customers visiting or employees working at residential premises. Ask your local council if permits are required, or if regulations exist which affect conducting business from a residential area.

Basic equipment and supplies

You will probably need to purchase or lease some basic equipment, including a personal computer (PC) to use for bookkeeping.

There are many suppliers of office and computer equipment, so shop around and be prepared to bargain for the best price or the most advantageous lease terms.

Do I need additional finance?

Your business plan should detail the amount of money ("capital") your business will require during its start-up phase and over the longer term.

You should have an accurate idea of how long it will take for the business to generate sufficient income so you can meet debts and support yourself. If you require additional finance, a number of options are available - such as a business or personal loan from a bank or lending institution. Consult your accountant or other business advisor for guidance on this.

Chapter 2

The Small Business Advantage

Small businesses are often perceived to be at a disadvantage when it comes to competing with larger companies.

Larger, more established businesses tend to have access to substantial capital. This allows more extensive marketing, dedicated personnel (professional, administrative and support), increased access to trade/industry information and discounts, and an ability to withstand a price-war or other competition.

But all is not lost. Small businesses tend to have a more flexible structure, lower overheads, a "hands-on" management that can detect subtle market changes and opportunities, and the authority to adapt to these changes quickly.

However, many small businesses do not make full use of these advantages, often because they fall victim to the stigma of "back-yard operator" attached particularly to home-based businesses.

Avoiding The Stigma

When running your own business from home, the image you project is very important. A professional image must be maintained at all times. This does not mean you must wear a suit and tie in your home office (although this may be appropriate for some businesses, especially if clients or business colleagues are likely to drop in).

However, it does mean that you must present yourself well and maintain the right attitude.

Stress The Advantages

A decade ago it was rare to find businesses that operated from residential premises. Many people treated such companies as poor cousins of their CBD relatives. The stigma attached to such business was that they offered inferior value or quality, or were "fly-by-nighters".

In the current business environment, this perception has all but disappeared. However, for various reasons, some people remain nervous about dealing with a home-based business.

If a client queries your work environment, be honest, but be sure to stress the benefits of working from home. These include:

Lower overheads mean reduced rates

This is always a client pleaser. Home-based businesses can minimise or avoid some potentially crippling costs (such as expensive CBD rents), and these savings can be passed on to the client in the form of competitive pricing for products and services.

Less office politics

If you work by yourself, or with a small team, office politics is unlikely to become an issue. As such, there is greater focus on the tasks at hand, and less time wasted waiting for approval or decisions from management.

Faster response time

Working from home often means fewer time-wasting distractions, (such as regular "unproductive" staff meetings) and the resulting productivity boost can translate into faster turnaround times.

> **TIP**
>
> *Avoid overstaffing. It might be tempting to hire extra staff to cover the workload when business picks up or if you win a large contract. But, before you do, consider whether the demand is long term, and if your business can support the additional staff if demand decreases. Other options are to employ part time or casual staff, or contract the additional work out to a third party.*

Personal attention

As a home-based worker, you are not "guarded" by secretaries or personal assistants. Clients can rest assured that they can talk to the person they want each time they call.

In addition, small businesses generally take on fewer clients than their larger competitors. This means more time and greater attention can be given to each project.

Enhance Your Image

To give your home office a more professional image, implement some or all of the following:

☐ Install a separate 'office' telephone line.

☐ Use an answering service when you are unable to answer the phone (for example, if you are in a meeting or out of the office).

☐ The area you live in is important, especially if clients will be calling on you. A well-regarded area is essential for a home business.

☐ Use a separate, clearly signposted entrance.

☐ Where possible, have a dedicated area set aside for clients. This area should be kept tidy and off limits to family members.

☐ Use professionally created letterheads and business cards.

The Timeshare Office

If you do not want clients to know that you work from home or consider it inappropriate to meet clients there, consider leasing space in a "timeshare" office complex. These are becoming more popular as small companies seek a CBD presence, while avoiding long-term leases and fit-out costs.

Timeshare offices have a central telephone and secretarial system. Each tenant has a unique telephone and facsimile number and office address. The receptionist answers the phone in the name of the company called.

Timeshare offices offer a number of benefits for both the home-based and mobile worker. These include:

☐ A central, prestigious place for meeting clients, complete with offices and meeting rooms.

☐ Dedicated or shared secretarial services (typing, filing and so on). The receptionist will take messages while you are out of the office, on holiday or away sick.

☐ A presence in the city, which allows you to mingle with clients and colleagues.

☐ An escape from the routine of home-life, especially when it is difficult to work at home (for example, if relatives are visiting).

These types of timeshare and serviced offices generally offer very flexible leasing arrangements (ranging from very short term to long term), and are becoming increasingly popular with small business owners who are reluctant to tie up much-needed capital in office leases.

Chapter 3

Your Home Office

You probably already know a number of people who work from home. They might be telecommuters or teleworkers, who use a spare room to complete office work at weekends. Others might "moonlight" in their spare time, and use a converted attic or garage for their projects. A few probably work full-time (or even part-time) for themselves from home.

Most home-based workers will admit they are happy with their working environment, and the flexibility, convenience and lifestyle it offers.

What they probably won't tell you, however, is how long it took them to make their home office productive, and the endless hours of frustration spent organising and reorganising it.

Setting up a home office isn't simply a matter of dragging a chair and desk near a telephone and sitting down to work. Establishing any office requires a lot of planning, and home offices - despite their occasional air of casualness - are no different.

This chapter examines the main elements of a home office. Although I concentrate primarily on home offices, many of the principles discussed are equally applicable to the establishment of other types of offices.

The Office

Your working area needs to be spacious, comfortable and functional. This may not sound difficult, but a surprising amount of detail is involved.

Follow these simple rules when planning your new work area:

Don't use shared areas

Your working environment should be a dedicated area, preferably with a door that can be closed to the other occupants of your home.

Avoid working in an area which must be shared with your partner or other householders (such as a bedroom), as this may lead to arguments (for example, when you need to work late at night and your partner wishes to sleep).

It is also not advisable to work and rest in the same room, so your mind can distinguish between the two "modes".

Avoid distractions

Your office should be free from distractions, so hallways and common rooms (such as the dining room) are out of the question.

Also, keep away from the main TV room and recreational areas, as these are bound to tempt your mind away from work.

Make it comfortable

There should be ample natural lighting (although a lamp can be used to provide additional light), as well as a means of controlling room temperature, such as an air-conditioner or heating unit.

Some rooms can become quite hot or cold during the day. Spend some time during normal working hours in the area you want to use as a home office, to estimate the temperatures you can expect. Do the same for noise levels. You might be surprised at how busy your street or neighbourhood is during the day!

The ideal area

The ideal area to use is a spare room, garage, attic or basement. If you are starting a new business, or if your home office is likely to be permanent, consider a purpose-built extension (although this may be too expensive at first). Before you invest in any extensions, check whether your local council allows home-based businesses - or you might find your new extension useless.

Be Professional

Once you have chosen a room or area in which to set up your home office, clear it of anything unrelated to work, such as books, beds, a stereo or a fridge.

While in your office, it is important to maintain a focused, professional attitude. Remove all indicators or reminders that you are, in fact, at home, to help achieve and maintain this attitude.

Office Layout

A mistake in office layout can result, at best, in inefficiency and inconvenience. At worst, it will require subsequent reorganisation (which can be costly if you have already installed electrical wiring and other fixtures). Plan your office carefully - if necessary draw a map (to scale) to make sure everything is satisfactory.

Electrical outlets

Be sure that sufficient power points are available for both your current needs (such as a heater, PC, printer and fax) and future needs (an extensive telephone system, printers, additional PCs, answering machine and so on).

If your budget permits, have additional power points installed by a qualified electrician, rather than relying on power extension cables and boards. As well as looking unprofessional, these can be dangerous and lead to frequent circuit overloads.

High-quality surge protection devices, which protect office equipment from lightning damage and other power spikes, are a must - especially if you live in an area prone to power fluctuations. Modems and facsimile machines are especially susceptible to power surge damage. Do not buy cheaper models of these machines - saving a few pounds in the short term might lead to disaster later.

If your work is particularly computer intensive, consider investing in an Uninterruptable Power Supply (UPS).

A UPS is essentially a high-tolerance power filter. It is generally box shaped and plugs directly into an ordinary power outlet. At the rear of the UPS are sockets into which you plug your electrical devices.

A UPS serves a dual purpose. It continuously filters the electricity supply to your equipment, absorbing any potentially harmful spikes or surges. In the event of a complete power failure, its internal batteries will provide around 10 minutes of power, giving you enough time to save your work and perform an orderly system shutdown.

UPSs are not cheap - a basic, good quality UPS costs about £200 - but then it only needs to save your PC from lightning damage once to pay its way.

When purchasing a UPS, advise the salesperson of the equipment you plan to use with it. Each UPS is designed to support a certain level of power use. Therefore, a UPS designed to protect a standard desktop PC and 15-inch monitor might not be appropriate for a larger PC with a 17-inch monitor. Be sure to buy one that will suit your equipment.

Telephone sockets

Your office should have its own telephone jack(s)/socket(s). Running extension cords from a telephone socket in another room is not advisable, for both aesthetic and safety reasons.

If your budget permits, install multiple telephone jacks to allow for future expansion.

Consider investing in one or more separate telephone lines and numbers for your home office. A separate telephone number will allow you to set up an answering service, and ensure that the phone is always answered in a professional manner. More importantly, it will mean that the telephone will not be tied up with personal calls when you are expecting important business ones.

Telephone services are covered in more detail in Chapter 4.

Desk and chair

Ensure that you have a comfortable desk and chair, as you will be spending a considerable amount of time using them.

Many people make the mistake of using old dining chairs, or other unsuitable seating, in a home office. These are uncomfortable to sit in for any length of time, and may lead to bad posture and possible back injury.

A good quality, ergonomically-designed chair can cost up to £500, but this is one area in which quality and comfort should be paramount.

Test the chair for height and comfort. Chairs that have an "S" shape are preferable, as these give good back support. Adjustability is also a key factor: the chair height, seat and back should all be adjustable. The chair should have arms, and these should be padded.

If possible, arrange to use the chair on a trial basis, to ensure that it suits your office environment. If you can't, test the chair in the showroom with a desk of similar proportions to yours - a mismatched desk and chair is a recipe for misery!

Your desk should be large enough to accommodate both an in-tray and out-tray, as well as your telephone handset and (if necessary) a computer monitor and printer. Again, you may not have all of these items yet, but always plan with an eye to the future. Few things kill productivity as effectively as an overcrowded desk!

Ideally, position your desk in a corner, with a side bureau beside it, to form an L-shape. This allows you to keep important office items on your desk (phone, PC and so on) while less important items (such as the fax and printer) are still within reach.

When positioning your desk, ensure it is near several spare electrical sockets, as well as plenty of lighting (natural light is preferrable).

Storage compartments

If you have spent your working life in a large office with dedicated administrative staff, you may not appreciate the need for a well-organised filing system.

The key to this is planning.

You will need a filing cabinet, or similar storage unit. If you think that you only need a one- or two-drawer cabinet, be sure to buy one with three or four drawers, so you have room for expansion. In the meantime you can use the spare drawers to store important items such as computer manuals, disks, printing paper, letterheads and so on.

Next, you will need to devise an effective filing system. To do this, try to anticipate the types of paperwork your office will generate. Find places for invoices, receipts, correspondence and purchase orders.

Your life will be considerably easier if you develop scrupulous filing habits (at least once a week) or your in-tray will soon overflow!

Mobile fittings

Mobile office furniture (such as chairs with wheels) is preferable to fixed furniture as it provides greater flexibility in rearranging your office.

Computer, telephone and facsimile

Buying the right office equipment and software can make or break a business.

In the chapters that follow we examine issues that should be addressed when buying computers, printers, faxes, modems and other important electronic accessories.

Chapter 4

Your Telephone System

When you set about designing, planning and establishing your new office, your telephone system may seem the least of your priorities. However, the humble telephone is one of the most important of all business tools. It can literally make or break your business.

If you think I am overstating the importance of the telephone, recall the number of times you have hung up in frustration when trying to contact a business.

How many times have you judged a firm's professionalism solely on the basis of your first attempt at telephone contact? Being put on hold and "lost", accidentally disconnected, diverted to a wrong extension - or worse, not having your call answered at all - are infuriating experiences and indications of an inadequate phone system.

Keep in mind that buying an inexpensive system that is not up to scratch will cost you much more in the long run than buying a more expensive but efficient system.

In this chapter, we explore the issues you should consider before committing yourself (and your money) to a phone system.

A Marriage Of Convenience

When considering a telephone system, note both the features of the system itself, and the benefits offered by your preferred telephone service provider. Marrying the two successfully can benefit you significantly.

For instance, many business phones now have a "one button solution" for call waiting. If you have an incoming call while you are already talking on the telephone, simply excuse yourself, press the call waiting button, and take the next call. In the meanwhile, your first caller is placed on hold and hears music - simple yet professional.

> # TIP
>
> *The first contact you will have with most potential clients is by telephone. Your telephone system is therefore often all that stands between you and a poor image.*

A Separate Business Telephone

If you can afford it, avoid using a single telephone number for both home and office use. There are a number of reasons for this:

Home vs the office

It is important to be able to distinguish between being at home and being in the office.

This can be especially difficult for home-office workers, given that this is one and the same place. Having an "office" telephone that must be answered in a professional manner will help you remain focused.

Avoid interruptions

Sharing a telephone number between home and business can lead to interruptions by personal phone calls during the day. These can be distracting and tie up the phone unnecesarily.

A professional approach

If you use the same telephone for personal and business calls, you might find that late-night or after-hours business calls are answered in a less-than-professional manner.

A separate business line can be diverted to an answering service or answering machine to take care of after-hours calls, maintaining a professional image at all times, and allowing you to relax once you have finished work.

Practical considerations

Using a home telephone line for business makes it difficult to maintain records of business calls for tax purposes. A separate business phone line makes it easier to maintain records and justify tax deductions.

Also, business telephone lines receive priority over residential lines when it comes to maintenance. So, the little extra you pay for a business line may mean the difference between same-day service or several days with a faulty phone line!

Phone Lines

Most houses are equipped with "twisted pair" wiring. This means two telephone lines are available, but, by default, only one is activated for use.

Activating and linking the second line to a separate telephone number is quite cheap (around £90). However, if you anticipate receiving a large number of calls each day, or if you also require access to a fax machine or modem, consider installing several additional lines.

An average home office requires at least two telephone lines, preferably three. One is used by your office telephone, one for a facsimile machine and one for modem use (or as a second telephone line).

If you don't plan to use the Internet or other online services extensively, you may be able to share one telephone line between your fax machine and modem.

Alternatives To Separate Lines

If you cannot afford to install additional telephone lines, consider using services that help to camouflage this fact.

Fax switches

If your budget is tight, or if there are delays installing extra phone lines, consider using a fax switch to share a single line between your telephone and fax machine.

A fax switch is a small device that plugs directly into your telephone wall socket, and incorporates two telephone jacks (which are used by your telephone and fax machine).

The fax switch monitors all incoming calls, listening for a telltale fax CNG tone (a half-second beep which most fax machines emit). If it detects this tone, it will automatically switch the incoming call to the fax machine. Otherwise, the call will proceed to the telephone as normal.

Unfortunately, some models do a less than professional job of switching. There can be a delay of a few seconds between the detection of an incoming call and the switch deciding what type of call it is. This delay is usually masked by a "ringing" tone generated by the fax switch or, on cheaper models, silence. Both can confuse human callers, and are a dead give-away to anyone who has experience with telephone systems.

Line sharers

Another alternative to installing multiple lines is to use a line sharer. This allows you to connect several devices (such as a telephone, fax machine and answering machine) to one telephone line.

In a similar manner to fax switches, line sharers detect the nature of the incoming call, and route it to the appropriate device. Incoming faxes are sent to the fax machine. Incoming calls are sent to the phone and, if unanswered, are diverted to the answering machine.

Line sharers are a cheap and practical alternative to multiple lines, and can be purchased at most electronics shops.

They are generally "smarter" than fax switches; for instance, if you answer a phone call from a fax machine by mistake, simply hang up and the switcher will automatically route the call to the fax machine. Line sharers can also handle two telephones on the same line, allowing you to manually forward calls to another extension, assuming you have two or more telephone lines.

More advanced models allow you to specify which line to use for outgoing calls. This can be handy if you live in an area in which several telephone service providers offer both local and international services. You can, for example, configure the line sharer to use one line for Mercury, and the other for BT, then use the service offering the cheapest rate for outgoing calls.

Distinctive ring

The distinctive ring service allows you to link several telephone numbers to one line.

For example, you might have a home number, business number and fax number linked to the one telephone line. The phone will emit a distinctive ringing sound for each number, so you can determine before you answer whether it is a personal, business or fax call, and act appropriately.

Some newer-model line sharers and fax switches can detect the distinctive ringing tones, and use these to route the phone calls automatically!

Choosing Your Telephone

Speakers

A speakerphone can be useful, especially if you share your office. This allows others to join in on conference calls, or listen in to important conversations.

Hands-free

If you spend a lot of time on the telephone, you may find a headset useful. This looks similar to a walkman or personal stereo earphone set, but includes a microphone to talk into.

Headsets allow you to use your hands while talking on the telephone, so you can enter data on your PC or take notes. They also help avoid neck cramps which can occur when you cradle the telephone with your neck and shoulder while performing such tasks.

Always try telephone headsets on for size. Be sure you are comfortable with the weight, and that it is fully adjustable. Models that can be easily detached from the phone system, allowing you to move about the office in between or during calls, are also useful.

Use the demonstration headset to make several calls before buying, to ensure the equipment has a good quality microphone and earphones.

Mute function

Mute keys can be a godsend - especially if you are working in a busy or noisy home office.

When depressed, mute keys allow you to hear the caller, while blocking the transmission of all sound from your end. This also allows you to hold a conversation with a co-worker while on the phone, or simply to block out noise.

Conference calls

Conference features only work on telephone systems which have more than one line. In essence, this feature allows you to link the caller on the first line with the caller on the second line, allowing both to speak to you and to each other at the same time.

TIP

If you are using a speakerphone, always advise the other party of this and mention if other listeners are present!

Intercom

If your office consists of several rooms, or if you use the same phone system for both home and business purposes, an intercom can prove useful.

An intercom allows the person who answers an incoming call to alert a co-worker in a different room without having to raise her/his voice. It is also handy for communicating between rooms, even if there are no calls waiting.

TIP

Cordless phones, like mobile phones, are susceptible to eavesdropping. To minimise the risk of calls being monitored, buy a digital cordless phone, rather than an analogue one. Some cordless phones also offer "scrambling" features, so anyone attempting to listen in will only hear garbled noises.

Volume/ringer control

Using volume control you can make the phone ring louder or softer, which can be handy if you are in a different room from the office.

The ringer control feature allows you to choose from a range of distinctive rings. Giving your office phone a different ring to your home phone will help avoid confusion.

Status lights

These are generally only handy if you have more than one phone. Status lights tell you at a glance whether someone is on hold, and which lines are in use.

Cordless phones

If you are looking for mobility and flexibility within the office, cordless telephones are ideal.

A cordless telephone works in conjunction with a base station, which relays telephone calls to the handset, and acts as a recharger (most cordless telephone handsets use rechargeable batteries).

To avoid static or other electrical interference, select a model with a transmission strength of at least 1000 metres.

This might seem excessive (unless you live in a mansion) but the transmission distance specified by the manufacturer is usually measured under ideal circumstances.

Walls, metal structures, electrical wiring and electrical equipment can interfere with transmission distance, with the result that "real life" distances are often considerably shorter than advertised.

Your cordless telephone will probably offer all the features you would expect from a desk-bound telephone - such as speakerphone, auto-redial, speed dialling and so on.

A Word Of Warning

Do not buy a cordless system to the exclusion of a standard phone system. Most cordless phones (and even some desk models) will not work during a blackout, as they do not draw power from the telephone line (as standard telephones do). Therefore, always have a backup phone handset for temporary use.

An ideal system is the combination of a desk-bound and cordless telephone.

My own telephone system (purchased for around £150) has a base station with a telephone handset, which also works in conjunction with a cordless telephone. I keep the base station in the office for normal use and the cordless extension in the living room so that I can take calls from anywhere in the house.

Telephone Services

Before purchasing, ask your telephone service provider for advice on which models work best with its system, and whether specific models can take advantage of any advanced services on offer.

Contact the corporate sales department of your service provider for explanatory literature and pricing.

Call forwarding

Call forwarding allows users to specify a telephone number to which incoming calls will be transferred if they are not answered or the line is in use.

For example, if you plan to be away from your office, you can have all calls to your office telephone number forwarded to your mobile phone, so you can answer calls wherever you are. The same system can be used to route faxes to a different office.

Call forwarding generally offers three options:

Forward on busy

If your number is engaged, calls are automatically forwarded to a second number (for example, an answering service or a different extension).

Delay forwarding

Calls not answered within a certain number of rings are forwarded to a specified telephone number.

This is handy for calls received after office hours, which can be forwarded from your office to your home phone.

Delay forwarding will also forward calls to an answering service if you cannot take them. Delaying the forwarding until the phone has rung several times gives you a chance to answer if you are in the office but away from your desk.

Programmable call forwarding

This allows you to turn call forwarding on or off at any time, and to determine the number to which the call should be forwarded. This is useful when you are out of your office at different times and for varying periods. Simply divert calls to your mobile or car phone and turn the diversion off when you return.

Call waiting

Call waiting allows a single telephone line to service two calls. When call waiting is activated, a short beep will sound if there is an incoming call while you are already speaking on the telephone. You can either ignore the call, or put your first caller on hold while you take the incoming call.

Some people dislike call waiting, as it can look cheap (can't the business afford two lines?) and portray a poor image. It is therefore preferable to use call waiting together with call forwarding.

If you have both activated, call forwarding will override call waiting. Therefore, if a second call is received while you are using the telephone, it will automatically be forwarded to

TIP

Call waiting can interfere with modem and facsimile machines. Because these devices exchange data using audio tones, the call waiting alert 'beep' can interfere with transmission. Therefore, disable call waiting on telephone lines used by these devices.

the service you have chosen (such as voice mail or an answering service).

This means that if you are in the middle of an important call or don't wish to inconvenience your first caller, you can ignore the incoming call and allow it to be diverted.

The Complete Beginner's Guide to Windows 95

This book isn't for the sort of people who get all frisky at the thought of a new operating system. They're already running Windows 95 and have been since day one. As the title suggests, it is for beginners:

- ❏ If you've just bought a new PC it will almost certainly be running Windows 95. You may need a helping hand to get started, and this book will serve as your introduction to Windows 95.
- ❏ If you've been using a PC with DOS or an earlier version of Windows and have decided to take the step up to Windows 95 this book will be a steadying hand to the new and to the different.
- ❏ If your office, school or college requires you to use a Windows 95 computer, this book will quickly show you the basics so you can get on with your work.
- ❏ Even if you're already using Windows 95 but simply want to do more with it, this book will teach you some neat tricks.

ISBN: 1-873668-28-7

Price: £4.95

About the Author

David Flynn is closely connected with Microsoft through his computer consultancy activities and is currently beta-testing early versions of the next Windows upgrade.

The Complete Beginner's Guide to Windows 95 is a low-cost, easy to understand guide, specially designed for everyone who hates wading through hundreds of pages of information to find a simple answer.   **Order form on page 94**

Chapter 5

ISDN
Technology

Integrated Services Digital Network (ISDN) technology is useful for both small and large businesses - especially those that place a premium on communications technology.

ISDN isn't very popular, yet, in the UK, largely as a result of two factors. Primarily, BT have only just started marketing the advantages of ISDN over standard telephone systems and, secondly, it can be expensive.

It may sound "chicken-and-egg", but the cost of ISDN in the UK is prohibitive, because its use is not widespread. However, in countries where ISDN services are entrenched, such as the USA, ISDN technology is almost on a par in terms of cost and availability with a standard telephone service.

As more businesses adopt ISDN technology, therefore, costs should decrease significantly.

What is ISDN?

ISDN technology allows one standard telephone line to be converted into three digital phone lines. These can be used to concurrently send faxes and data (such as computer files or videoconferencing images), and to make voice-based telephone calls.

Using a single telephone line, therefore, you can make telephone calls, send and receive faxes and use a PC-based videoconferencing application or the Internet - all at the same time!

ISDN systems can, of course, be used to make and receive ordinary phone calls, and the sound quality of these is greatly enhanced.

Telecommuting with ISDN

If you telecommute, ISDN offers several benefits - especially if you need to access the computer network at head office.

With an ISDN connection, you can access files and other network-based peripherals as if you were sitting at a computer in the office. There is no noticeable delay as files and other material are sent to your computer, as often occurs with standard modem connections.

This means you can manipulate files in real time, send and receive office email and so on. Thanks to ISDN, being a "remote user" does not equate to a loss in productivity.

More importantly, the same line you use to access the head office's computer network can be used as a telephone line (so your co-workers can call you) as well as a fax line or - if you would normally attend a number of meetings - a videoconferencing line.

Speed is the key

The data transfer speeds available via ISDN are many times faster than those offered by today's fastest modems.

This means you can access advanced Internet resources (such as electronic news and Internet video conferencing), as well as other computer networks, without the delays caused by slower modems.

Installing ISDN

ISDN is neither cheap nor easy to install and configure. The best advice is to leave this to an ISDN specialist or your telephone service provider.

Your house or office may need special wiring, although ISDN equipment generally works well with existing wiring. The ISDN consultant or your telephone service provider can advise you on this.

Benefits of ISDN

ISDN has three key uses for a SOHO or telecommuter:

Access to the Internet

ISDN provides high-speed Internet access, supporting a data transfer rate considerably higher than that of current modem hardware. If you wish to host your own Web server or obtain a permanent Internet connection (for example, if you use the Internet to sell your products and services), ISDN is almost essential.

Advanced voice services

A number of voice services usually available through third party providers can be used in conjunction with ISDN technology. ISDN also allows you to set up your own voicemail and teleconferencing systems.

Remote access & videoconferencing

As mentioned earlier, an ISDN connection offers telecommuters fast, reliable access to data stored on their employer's computer system.

ISDN can also be used to host videoconferencing facilities, allowing you to "sit in" on meetings with colleagues.

In addition, ISDN technology offers services similar to those available via standard telephone systems, such as hold, three-way conference calls and call transfers.

Cost Savings

If a high percentage of your calls are made to overseas locations, you can achieve some savings with ISDN (which uses a different billing system to the standard phone system).

Ask for full details of the charges involved, as most ISDN services are charged *per second.*

Before You Invest

Before you invest in ISDN, discuss the following issues with your telephone service provider or ISDN consultant:

❑ What are the basic costs involved in getting an ISDN connection (that is, the hardware, setup and labour costs)? What will I be charged for using the service (monthly rental and access charges)?

❑ Is there a recommended/preferred supplier of equipment?

❑ How does ISDN-based technology compare - both in terms of cost and efficiency - with a standard telephone connection?

❑ What options are available for future expansion?

❑ Have they recently installed a similar system for someone else? Can I contact this person to discuss his or her assessment of the system?

Chapter 6

Mobile Phones

Mobile telephony is a driving force in 1990s business communication. And the British have embraced mobile telephony with a fondness not witnessed in other nations, even the USA. As a result of this widespread use, fees and equipment costs have dropped significantly in the past few years.

It is now possible to buy a reliable mobile telephone for under a hundred pounds, making it standard equipment for most SOHOs.

How Mobile Phones Work

Basically, a mobile phone consists of a built-in receiver and transmitter.

When your mobile phone is on, its transmitter is in constant contact with the nearest base station, sending it signals several times a second.

The base station routes incoming telephone calls from the standard telephone network to your mobile phone, and transmits outgoing calls to the standard exchange.

By maintaining contact with the nearest base station, the location of your mobile phone can be pinpointed when the base station needs to route incoming calls to it.

When you use your mobile phone, its transmitter relays your voice to the base station. From here it is routed to the nearest major telephone exchange, and transmitted along normal telephone lines to the other party's telephone.

Conversely, when the other party speaks, his or her voice is carried across the standard telephone network to the exchange and then over the airwaves to the base station nearest your mobile phone, which broadcasts it to your receiver.

The quality of the reception depends on how far you are from the nearest base station, the surrounding terrain (mountains, hills and rivers can cause interference) and the number of users the base station is serving at the time of your call.

The country is divided into geographical areas called "cells", each of which is serviced by one or more base stations.

If you are travelling while using your mobile phone, you may move between cells served by different base stations. The switching between them is automatic and instantaneous, so your conversation is not interrupted.

Types of Mobile Phones

Two types of mobile phones are currently available: analogue and digital. Analogue is an older, cheaper technology. Digital is more recent, and looks set to become the dominant mobile phone technology worldwide.

Benefits of digital over analogue

Unlike analogue, the digital mobile phone network is here to stay and also offers several benefits, including:

❏ Clearer reception.

❏ Enhanced privacy.

❏ Easier "roaming" with other networks.

Some of these issues are examined below:

Privacy

The issue of privacy should not be treated lightly. It is surprisingly easy to eavesdrop on an analogue mobile phone - you will no doubt recall the infamous "Squidgygate" recordings of the Late Princess Diana's mobile telephone conversations. Using a cheap radio scanner (which can be bought at most electronics shops) anyone can listen in on analogue mobile phone conversations.

If you work in a competitive industry, or frequently hold confidential conversations with friends, clients or associates, then the only serious choice is a digital mobile phone.

Summary and Recommendation

If price is not an issue, and the digital network coverage in your area is satisfactory, buy a digital mobile phone. If you are working to a budget, and are not too worried about privacy, take advantage of the bargains offered on analogue mobile phones.

Car Kits

If you spend a lot of time in the car, make sure your mobile phone comes with a car kit, or can be fitted with one.

A car kit allows your mobile phone's receiver to be temporarily connected to your car stereo system, so that the callers's voice can be heard through the car speakers. The kit usually includes a bracket to hold your mobile phone, allowing hands-free use.

Car kits often include a separate, more powerful antenna. This is useful if you are in a rural area where reception is patchy, or if you are moving from cell to cell.

Types Of Mobile Phones

'Bricks'

This is the unflattering name given to older-style mobile phones, which are similar in size, shape and weight to a brick!

These inexpensive phones are mainly available second-hand, and can only be used on the analogue network. They are not as convenient as smaller, more modern models, but are light enough to be carried in a briefcase or toolbox, or tucked away in your glove box.

Hand-helds

Hand-helds are the most common type of mobile phone.

They range from trouser-pocket size to purse and shirt-pocket size, and most can be clipped onto a belt or diary. Recent models are so light that their weight is measured in grams!

Many hand-helds are sold with several types of detachable aerials (long ones for stronger reception, short ones for use in metropolitan areas) and are easily used with car kits.

Choosing A Mobile Phone

Consider the following features when choosing a mobile phone:

Size

This can be an important consideration. Is the phone easy to carry and store?

TIP

Consider the safety implications of using a hand-held mobile phone in your car. It can cause distractions and lead to accidents. As recent legal cases have shown, even if you don't kill yourself, you could end up in jail for injuring someone else. Whatismore, it is conceivable laws will be passed in the near future, prohibiting their use. So it makes sense to get a hands-free set now and save having to change later on.

Ergonomics

Does the phone fit comfortably in your hand? Are the buttons legible and easy to press? Does it "suit your face" (that is, can you hold it to your ear and talk easily into the microphone)?

Weight

Is its weight suitable for your intended use? For example, it may be inconvenient to carry a "brick" in your briefcase if you spend most of the day walking around.

On the other hand, if you spend a lot of time in your car or office, buying the lightest phone available might not be a priority - especially since the smaller and lighter a mobile phone, the more expensive it is likely to be.

Battery life

How much "talk time" is available before the phone needs to be recharged? How long is its standby life (when it is turned on, but not being used)?

If you use your mobile phone frequently, a longer "talk time" is more important than a long standby life (you can always recharge the phone overnight).

Alternatively, if you use your telephone less often, but don't always have access to power outlets (say, because you are a travelling salesperson), a longer standby period might suit you. Some phones can operate for four days on "standby" without needing to recharge.

Ringer

Can you change the volume of the ringer? Can you select different styles of rings? Does the phone offer a "vibrating" alternative (where it vibrates instead of ringing when there is an incoming call)?

Some venues (such as restaurants) frown upon the intrusive noise mobile phones make. The ability to turn the ringer volume down or off can be a godsend during meetings or at social functions.

Equally, if your mobile phone ringer is too quiet, you might not hear it over the roar of an engine, or if you are in a separate room.

Night use

Is the phone's display backlit for night use?

Retractable antenna

Some models of mobile phones use fixed antennas, which can make them difficult to stow.

Models with shorter antennas (but no appreciable loss in signal strength) or retractable antennas are preferable.

Timers

Many models display the length of the most recent call on-screen, enabling you to keep a record for billing purposes or expenses.

Locking

Once a mobile phone is "locked" (by keying in a numeric code), it cannot be operated until the code is keyed in again.

This prevents anyone from using your phone to make calls in your absence, or if the phone is lost or stolen.

Sound quality

How loud is the earpiece? Can you hear the caller above the noise in a crowded room?

Be sure to test this before you buy the phone. Simply dial any number on a demonstration model. As it won't yet be connected to a service provider, you should receive a recorded message advising you that the phone is not yet operational. How easily can you hear this message?

Mobility

Can the phone be used in conjunction with a notebook PC or modem to send faxes or connect to the Internet? (These types of phones tend to be more expensive). If so, do you need any special cables, attachments or software?

Display size

Is the display easy to read?

Warranty

How long is the manufacturer's warranty? What does the warranty cover? Is there an extended warranty option and, if so, how much does it cost? Does the warranty cover additional items such as the second battery, car kit and battery recharger?

A surprising number of mobile phones break as a result of being dropped, knocked off desks, or having coffee spilt on them. Be sure to find out which "mishaps" are covered, and whether you will be given a replacement phone while yours is being repaired.

Repair agents

Is there a local repair agent, or must the phone be sent back to the makers?

Additional Options

Investigate additional options offered by the phone and/or service provider, even if you have no immediate use for them.

Enhanced security features

Among these are the ability to "lock" stored telephone numbers, as well as PIN-only access to voicemail services.

Advanced calling features

These include call waiting, call diversion and voicemail, as well as the ability to store phone numbers in memory for speed dialing.

Alphanumeric paging

This allows a mobile phone to receive and display paging messages in text form.

Rapid recharging/discharging

Some batteries develop a "memory" if they are recharged without being fully discharged, and this can decrease the length of the battery's life.

Having a fast discharge option allows you to drain the battery completely before each recharging.

Any key answering

This allows you to answer an incoming call by pressing any key.

Signal strength indicator

The signal strength indicator, which appears on the phone's display, shows how "strong" the signal from the nearest base station is. Higher signal strength means better call quality.

Call restriction

Using this feature you can restrict the types of calls that can be made from the phone. For example, you might restrict usage to local calls only, or allow long distance calls but block overseas calls.

Summary

When you purchase a mobile phone, you are essentially paying for convenience. The more convenience a phone offers, the more expensive it will be.

Smaller mobile phones are easier to carry and store. Longer battery life means less "down time" recharging your batteries. Stronger signal strength means fewer interruptions and clearer reception.

If you depend on your mobile phone daily for business communications, investing in this kind of "convenience" is essential.

Pricing Traps

Mobile phones are now very reasonably priced. As mentioned earlier, it is possible to find a good analogue or digital phone for around £50, compared with £500 or more a few years ago.

The reason for this decrease in price relates to the commission paid by telephone service providers to mobile phone retailers and (lack of) demand.

If you were to buy a mobile phone from a retailer without signing up with a particular telephone service provider (such as BT, Orange or Vodafone), you would probably pay hundreds of pounds more than the advertised price.

This is because the retailer receives a commission (which can amount to several hundred pounds) from the telephone service provider you sign up with.

In addition, the retailer generally also receives a small percentage of every penny you spend in calls made from your mobile phone (which could amount to thousands of pounds over the lifetime of your phone).

It is therefore in the retailer's interest to sell as many mobile phones as possible (even if there is little profit on the actual phone, or it is sold at a loss), in order to maximise the number of people signed up.

It is important to understand how this arrangement between the retailer and service provider affects you.

Firstly, it means you are in a good position to negotiate on price. If a retailer thinks that you are seriously interested in buying a particular model, he may sell it to you at less than the advertised price if this is necessary to "make the sale". After all, the majority of retailers make their profit from commissions rather than the sale price.

Secondly, this arrangement means that you should thoroughly investigate the services offered by the telephone service provider, rather than relying on the recommendation of a salesperson (who is likely to have a financial interest in the outcome of your decision).

Finally, do not simply accept a dealer's recommendation on a model. The retailer may recommend models that are in stock (in order to close the deal and make the commission), instead of a model that suits your needs.

Special Deals - Or Are They?

Almost every day telephone service providers advertise "special deals" which offer seemingly unbeatable value. For a minimal cost, they say, you can get a new phone and quick access to mobile telephony.

As with most advertised specials, caveat emptor ("let the buyer beware") is the guiding rule: it really does pay to read the fine print.

Advertisers are now obliged to advise consumers of the total cost of special deals advertised with mobile phone purchases. If you look closely, you will find that some of these "specials" are not so special after all!

For instance, many advertisements offer mobile phones for less than the off-the-shelf price. To take advantage of this promotion, however, you may need to register with one of the mobile phone service providers, agreeing to "lock yourself in" with that provider for a set period (sometimes up to three years).

In additon, you agree to pay a set monthly subscription rate (or "tariff"), which is often much higher than the lowest rate available. In effect, the cost of the higher than normal tariff and/or set-period contract subsidises the price of the phone. You are not really getting a bargain at all!

Most special offers state (in the fine print, of course) that if you decide to change to another telephone service provider, or to register for a cheaper tariff, you must pay the full cost of the mobile phone (or a penalty figure, which can amount to several hundred pounds).

In short, do your sums. You will often be better off paying more for your mobile phone, but signing up for a lower monthly subscription without a set-period contractual obligation.

Towards the Future

Mobile telephones are an essential business tool - you simply cannot beat the flexibility they offer, especially when you are on the move. But making telephone calls from your mobile phone can be expensive.

There is a cheaper alternative, which has only recently become available in Europe. Known generically as personal communicators, these look similar to a standard mobile phone, but offer an ingenious twist.

When used in your home or office, a personal communicator accesses the standard telephone system (in much the same way as a cordless phone does), which means that calls cost the same as a standard call. Once you leave the home or office, however, it automatically switches into mobile mode, using the mobile telephone network (and calls are charged accordingly). This way, you can use the same telephone wherever you are!

Exciting technology - keep an eye out for it.

⇨ Continued from page 4

DISK 6 - Smart Address

Address-management system with great-looking interface (complete with tabbed-windows and toolbar with tooltips) and full of features. It links directly to any word processor; has mail-merge data file creation for Microsoft Word; offers modem support so any phone number can be dialed directly; can print envelopes and labels; has mail-sort capabilities and sophisticated search capabilities; and offers reminder systems and callbacks. Unlike some other address programs, Smart Address lets you customize nearly every aspect of the program. Wizards help with importing and exporting of data. Uses the Windows Multiple Document Interface (MDI) so several address books can be open at once. System Requirements: Windows 95

DISK7 - SmartSum

Easy-to-use talking calculator that uses PC-speaker or sound-card audio to announce digits, operations, and results. You can save and reload calculations, change display accuracy, add notes to data entries, record macros, and inject results automatically into other applications. SmartSum also offers tax calculations, 10 memories for more-complex calculations, and a printed tally using any available font. System Requirements: Windows 3.1x.

Perfect Keyboard for Windows 95/NT

Automatically replaces keystroke combinations or text with phrases that you define, such as the date and time. You organize the types of key combinations/replacements in a File Manager-style dialog, adding new categories with an icon designated for that subject. Options let you choose a character, such as the space bar, to trigger a replacement. A Find Shortcut function lets you view your library to remind yourself of your choices. System Requirements: Windows 95.

DISK8 - SDSS Spreadsheet

Supports single document (sheet) applications. Simple and fast, SDSS supports 125 function calculations and data manipulation features found in commercial spreadsheets. SDSS can read and save in Visual Tools 1.0 (VTS), Microsoft Excel 4.0 (XLS), and tab-delimited text files. Consider this a Notepad of spreadsheets: small, fast and safe. The online help file is well organized and easy to use. System Requirements: Windows 3.1x.

DISK9 - Activity Log

Useful for anyone working with a variety of projects. It allows you to track the length of time you spend working on a particular project as well as the tasks completed during your work sessions. Several projects can be monitored at the same time. Activity Log will also add your time, allowing you to start and stop ongoing projects and those performed over a long period of time. . System Requirements: Windows 95.

AdMaker

Lets you design small-business ads using fonts, clip art, drawings, and colored text in bold, italic, or underlined styles. You can create simple and impressive ads with the program's WYSIWYG format. Choose one of 14 colors for messages that can be rotated up to 90 degrees. Add pizzazz with BMP, PCX, or WMF images. Draw lines, boxes, or circles of varying sizes, outlined or filled with color. Requirements: Visual Basic 3.0 runtime module (incl.) and Windows 3.1x.

Bob's Macros

Set of more than 140 macros for Microsoft Excel versions 4 and 5. The macros automate many common and/or time-consuming tasks, increasing user productivity. Some of the macros let you save/close all files; insert date, time, and filename in the active worksheet; draw boxes; and transpose rows and columns without losing the cell references. . System Requirements: Excel and Windows 3.1x.

DISK10 - PlanMagic Business

Contains a series of documents and spreadsheets that run within Microsoft Word for Windows to help you organize a comprehensive business plan. A Help file describes use of each of the 11 modules, which include plan, profit and loss, balance sheet, statistical data, investment budget, organizational structure, sales, cash flow, profit and loss forecasts, time table, and a graphical presentation. Some information is omitted and some documents are password-protected to encourage registration. System Requirements: Word for Windows 6.x and Windows 3.1x.

Paramind Brainstorming Program

An interesting and unique program designed to help you brainstorm ideas. The program uses the TWIE (telical word interaction exhaustion) linguistic idea as an idea multiplier, or as a tool for visualizing detailed concepts or ideas. You simply enter your ideas through the keyboard or by importing text through the clipboard. The program then replaces words or fills in ideas to help you think in new ways. System Requirements: Windows 3.1x.

Order form on page 96

Chapter 7

Answering

Machines

I CAN CERTAINLY TAKE THE MESSAGE

Most new small businesses cannot afford to hire someone to answer telephones on a full or even part-time basis. Given the variety of small business life, you also cannot guarantee that you will always be on hand to answer the telephone. A sensible alternative is an answering machine.

Installing

Answering machines are easy to install. Simply plug in the power adapter and connect the cable supplied to the jack used by your telephone. You might need to buy a double adapter for the jack if one is not supplied with the answering machine.

Your answering machine should be configured by default to automatically answer incoming calls after a set number of rings, (usually between two and four, which gives you enough time to answer the call if you are in the office). After playing your brief recorded message, callers will be prompted to leave a message for your attention.

Recording a message

Recording the message is probably the hardest aspect of setting up your answering machine.

Depending on the model, you will probably have to press the record button once to start recording and then press the record or stop button to finish. The tape will rewind, and your message will be played back to you.

Deciding what to say on your recorded message can be agonising.

Always clearly identify yourself and your company (refer to it by name). Remember that this message may be the first impression potential clients have of you and your company, so make it as professional as possible. Ask callers to leave their name and a contact telephone number, including the STD area code if appropriate. If you have a mobile phone, advise callers of the number and invite them to call you if the matter is urgent.

If recording your message makes you nervous, write it down and rehearse a few times. When recording, avoid long pauses and mispronounced words. Keep the background noise to a minimum, and speak clearly at your normal pace.

Types Of Answering Machines

Tape models

Most answering machines use small magnetic tapes to record the messages left by callers. These operate in a similar way to personal cassette players. Tape-based models are very affordable.

Tapeless models

Some newer models store messages on electronic computer memory chips, thereby avoiding the distortion that can occur when magnetic tapes get old.

Unfortunately, models that use memory chips offer less recording time (usually only between 15 and 20 minutes in total), but this should be sufficient if you review your messages daily.

Features

Most answering machines offer a host of useful features, such as:

Voice activation

Some tape-based answering machines only allow a caller to record a message within a set period of time before s/he is cut off. To avoid this problem, choose a model with voice-activation.

These models only record once the caller begins to speak, and continue recording until s/he stops. This feature also filters out hang-up tones, which occur when the caller hangs up without leaving a message. This conserves recording time (important on tapeless models) and reduces the time you must spend listening to messages.

Time and date stamps

Newer model answering machines use an internal clock to record the time and date a message was left. Before each message is played, a voice provides you with this information.

Remote retrieval

Some models allow you to retrieve and play back your messages remotely. This means you can ring your answering machine and have it play back your messages over the telephone, no matter where you are.

This feature can be invaluable for people who are frequently away from the office. As a security measure, you generally have to dial a three or four digit passcode or play a tone generated by a special keyring before you can access your stored messages.

Message forwarding

Some newer models can be programmed to call you at a predetermined telephone number (such as your mobile phone) to advise you when someone has left a message. These models will also play back messages once they have contacted you.

Dual lines

Make sure your answering machine can answer two telephone lines - this will be handy when your office expands!

Chapter 8

Using a Pager and Voicemail

Some people prefer pagers to mobile telephones. Pagers are less obtrusive - they do not ring loudly or "demand" to be answered. Therefore, they are unlikely to interrupt a conversation or business meeting, or drag you away from clients to take a call.

Furthermore, when used in conjunction with an answering service, pagers can project an image that your company is bigger than it really is.

Most answering services will answer incoming calls in your company name and with a specific greeting, giving callers the impression that they are a receptionist or secretary.

Using An Answering Service

Using an answering service is quite easy, and can be very cost effective. First, contact your telephone service provider to arrange for call-forwarding on your office telephone line.

Next, contact answering services in your area for quotes. If you have not already bought a pager, the answering service may offer a package in which you lease a pager and contract their services for a fixed monthly sum.

Once you have the contract in place, the rest is smooth sailing.

If a client calls your office number while you are out, the incoming call will be diverted to the answering service. This will occur either immediately or after a certain number of rings, depending on how you configure your call-forwarding service.

The answering service answers the call in your company name, advises that you are not available to take the call, and takes a message which includes the caller's details. The service then sends the caller's details via a radio transmitter to your pager.

If your pager is turned on, it will either vibrate or emit a short beep to alert you of the incoming message. You can then either return the client's call or contact the answering service to see if there is a more detailed message.

Newer, more expensive models - called alphanumeric pagers - can receive lengthy text messages. This means that the answering service can pass on messages in full!

Pricing

Paging and answering service providers offer various levels of service, with corresponding price structures.

Most paging services charge a flat monthly fee, which covers both pager rental and a set number of outgoing pages from the answering service. This basic service can be quite cheap, as long as you do not exceed the maximum number of pages. If you do, you are generally charged a premium rate for each extra page.

In addition to the basic monthly fee, you can "buy" additional pages in advance, at a discounted rate.

If you are starting a new business, you may find it difficult to determine the number of pages you will need each month. In this case, enter into a contract for the basic service for the first few months. Keep track of the number of pages you receive, and, once you have a better idea of your requirements, contact your service provider to work out the most cost-effective plan.

Voicemail Services

An increasingly popular alternative to pagers is voicemail. Voicemail operates in a similar manner to answering machines, but offers greater flexibility, without any up-front equipment costs.

Most telephone service providers now offer voicemail, which can be used with both standard and mobile phones. A basic voicemail service can cost as little as a few pounds a month (plus retrieval costs - but more on these later).

Getting started

To use voicemail you will need call forwarding activated on your mobile or office telephone (or both).

Once this has been arranged, contact your telephone service provider to discuss the costs of voicemail, and the level of service which will best suit your business.

Your next step is to call the voicemail service system. Your telephone service provider will give you contact numbers, and should provide an instruction booklet telling you how to use the service.

Voicemail services are provided by a computer system running special software, which enables it to answer telephone calls and play/record voice messages.

To configure your "voice mailbox" and record your message, call the voicemail computer and it will guide you through the setup process.

The setup process

First, you will generally be asked to state your name. This will be recorded and used in a welcome message when you contact the voicemail system in future.

Next, you will be prompted to record the message that will be played to all incoming callers. You can play back your message, and, if you are dissatisfied with it, record another.

Finally, you will be prompted to provide a PIN (usually a four-digit number). In future, when you contact the system, you will need to key in the PIN for identification before the system will play back stored messages.

To complete the process, your telephone must be configured to divert to the voicemail system (using call forwarding or diversion) when you are away from your office or do not answer the call within a specified number of rings.

When a call is diverted the voicemail system will answer it, play your recorded message and prompt callers to leave a message.

TIP

Some people use their voicemail to 'be lazy' and allow all calls to go onto the system. Then, when it suits them, they pick up their calls. Whilst this way of working can save you from interruptions, and can be used to screen calls, it is not to be recommended. Many callers simply do not like talking to 'machines' and will simply call one of your competitors. Others may find your lack of 'attention' as an indirect insult.

Retrieving voicemail

To retrieve your voicemail, simply call the telephone number you were given by the voicemail service provider. Once you have proved that you own the voicemail box (usually by keying in your PIN), you can ask to hear your stored messages. After listening to each message, you have the option of either deleting it from the system or storing it for future playback.

Retrieval costs

Most voicemail systems charge for both the time callers spend recording messages (although this is usually only a few pence a minute) and the time you spend retrieving messages.

Not all telephone service providers have voicemail systems in every area and town. If you are in an area without local voicemail services, your voicemail will be stored on a computer in a different area with a different area code. This means that each time a call is forwarded from your office or mobile phone to your voicemail service, and each time you contact your voicemail to retrieve stored messages, you incur STD call rates!

Ask your voicemail service provider for details of all costs involved in your voicemail service.

Benefits of voicemail

Many people consider voicemail to be more personal than pagers, as the caller hears your voice explaining that you cannot take the call. It is also more flexible, as you can check for messages at any time, and from any telephone (or using your mobile phone).

You can also store messages permanently on your voicemail service, which is handy if you need to refer to a message left by a caller some time ago.

Voicemail systems can also be quite cheap to operate - certainly less than hiring a secretary, and generally cheaper than an answering service.

Chapter 9

Buying a Fax Machine

Facsimile machines have come a long way in a relatively short time. As recently as the 1970s and early 1980s the telex machine ruled the business roost. However, by the late 1980s, fax machines had taken their place and were regarded as indispensable business tools.

Even with the advent of online communications, video phones and group collaboration technologies, the fax machine is likely to monopolise interoffice communication for at least the next decade.

Therefore, a fax machine (or a device capable of sending and receiving faxes) is an essential part of the electronic office.

Choosing a Fax Machine

There are several types of fax machines available:

Thermal

Thermal fax machines use heat sensitive paper (which is easy to distinguish from ordinary paper by its glossy look and feel). The image of documents received is literally "burnt" onto the paper.

Thermal faxes need little maintenance and are cheap to run. When buying a thermal paper model, be sure to choose one with an automatic paper cutter. Thermal paper is purchased in rolls, and without an automatic paper cutter you will have to manually cut or tear each fax from the roll.

Plain paper

Plain paper faxes print on ordinary paper, such as that used in your printer or photocopier.

This offers potential savings, as plain A4 paper is considerably cheaper than thermal paper. In addition, you can buy paper in bulk for all your office needs.

Plain paper faxes operate very much like printers, offering both laser and inkjet quality - depending on how much you are prepared to spend.

The downside to plain paper faxes is that they are usually more expensive than their thermal counterparts.

Features To Look For

Speed

Most fax machines in use today cannot receive data at speeds greater than 9,600bps

Even if your fax machine is able to send data faster than this, it will have to slow down to the top speed of the other fax machine, as the two must synchronise to exchange data (which is what the fax machines are doing when they emit high-pitched squeals).

Therefore, it is rarely worth paying extra for a fax machine that can operate faster than 9,600bps, unless you plan to use it for a specific purpose. For example, if you regularly fax a client in a different country, you might both save on timed STD charges by investing in faster fax machines.

If you decide to do this, try to buy the same model fax machine as the person to whom you will be faxing. It is an industry quirk that different model fax machines may not be able to "talk" to one another at high speeds, even though they are both rated high-speed!

Resolution

Most fax machines (especially thermal models) cannot handle high print resolutions.

However, the resolutions they can achieve are fine for sending typed or neatly hand-written documents, or basic graphics, such as charts or graphs. Beyond this, however, you may have some difficulty obtaining quality detail.

Choose a fax machine that allows you to select the best resolution (or which automatically selects the best resolution) for the document being sent.

Most fax machines offer a fine mode, used for sending graphics or documents with very small type. Others offer a superfine mode for even clearer reproduction, but this feature tends to work only if the other fax machine is the same or a compatible model.

Contrast

Your fax machine should allow you to change the contrast (or darkness) of the facsimile.

This can be especially helpful when sending poorly photocopied documents or colour documents (which do not always fax well).

Optional Features

Your fax machine may also offer features such as:

Auto-redial

If the receiving fax machine is engaged, your fax machine will automatically attempt to resend the fax after waiting a specified period.

Delay faxing

Delay faxing can help keep STD fax charges to a minimum.

It allows you to program your machine to send a facsimile after office hours, taking advantage of cheaper long-distance rates.

This is also handy for faxing large or non-urgent documents without tying up your fax line during business hours.

Additionally, you can use delay faxing to send "bulk faxes", where the same fax is sent to numerous recipients (for instance, if you are faxing a price list to clients).

Document storage

Some faxes will scan the document you wish to fax, and store an image of it in internal memory (usually on a hard disk). This electronically-stored copy is then used for faxing.

This feature is useful when you want to send the same fax to multiple recipients. Simply run the document through the machine once, then enter the fax numbers of all the recipients. A copy of the fax will be sent to each number, without requiring you to re-feed the document each time.

More advanced models can use the internal memory to receive faxes when your machine runs out of paper -

a very handy feature if you are away from the office for any length of time.

Programmable memory

Most faxes allow you to store details of fax numbers you use frequently. This saves time, and decreases the likelihood of mistakes when dialling.

Advanced models allow you to program the numbers of several recipients into one key, making group faxing easy.

Tax Self Assessment Made Easy

Order form for all books on page 94

Chapter 10

Buying a Personal Organiser

Few offices would function well without a diary: a central repository of daily events, meetings, telephone numbers, "to do" lists and the like.

Recently, electronic diaries have come into their own. Although known by various names - such as Personal Digital Assistants (PDAs), Personal Organisers and Personal Information Managers (PIMs) - they all serve the same function; namely, storing often-used information in an easy-to-access format.

Early personal organisers were bulky and expensive, and had limited application. As the technology was perfected, size and price decreased - almost in proportion to increases in functionality!

Personal organisers now available range from cheaper (£25 - £50) models that have a reasonable storage memory, through to high-end large-memory models (which can cost over £500).

The cheaper models are useful for storing contact names, telephone numbers, meeting schedules and short messages. More expensive models offer features such as word processing and database functions, and top-of-the-range models can approach PCs in terms of functionality.

Most personal organisers can interface (via cable or infrared device) with a printer to print out stored text messages, database entries and so on.

Some have communication facilities, such as plug-in cards that, when connected to a mobile phone, allow users to send and receive email and faxes.

Many can synchronise with a PC, so schedules and contacts are at your fingertips, both in the office and on the road.

Why Buy a Personal Organiser?

Personal organisers have several advantages over paper-based diaries. Finding information in a database or contact list is easy using a personal organiser - simply type in a word (or partial word) and press the "search" key.

Better still, with a personal organiser you no longer need to search for a pen to make notes - you simply type them in.

Scheduling meetings is easy - and an alarm alerts you to them in advance. Short messages can be entered as electronic memos, which won't be lost or left in your pocket for the washing machine.

A personal organiser can store and retrieve all the daily information you memorise, record or jot down. Better still, your information is together, indexed and organised.

The Downside

For all their excellent features, personal organisers do have some disadvantages. Most of these can be avoided or minimised, however, by choosing a quality model, or one that suits your specific needs.

Miniature keypads

Unfortunately, size dictates that personal organisers have very small keyboards (or keypads), and entering data using only two fingers can be frustrating. If you are used to a PC keyboard the keys may seem very small and close together.

However, it is fair to say that most people get used to the size of the keypad.

Functionality = Weight

The more functions a personal organiser offers, the heavier it is likely to be. Organisers with plug-in memory expansion and modem cards, for example, can measure twice the length and thickness of a wallet. These are cumbersome, except when carried in briefcases or handbags.

Data loss

Soon your personal organiser will - and should - become the central repository of your office information. Few people realise just how important this information is until they lose it!

Dropping or jarring a personal organiser might not break it, but could cause the batteries to become dislodged, resulting in data loss. Batteries can also run down and may expire, catching you without replacements handy.

To avoid or minimise the potential of data loss follow these tips:

Use quality batteries

Replace batteries within the period recommended by the manufacturer. If you are not comfortable fitting batteries, ask the dealer to do it for you.

Back up

Choose a personal organiser that can transfer or back up its data to computer. It is always sensible to keep backups, especially of data you use regularly.

Buying a Personal Organiser

Before buying a personal organiser, examine the basic hardware, design and user interface it offers.

Your personal organiser should have:

A good quality screen

The screen should be capable of displaying at least four lines of legible text, and be backlit for night use.

Clear text display

There should be sufficient contrast between the text and screen so that text is clear and easy to read.

Quality keypad

The keys should be clearly marked and comfortable to use. Buying a model with a QWERTY keyboard layout, which is standard for computer keyboards, will help you remember where keys are.

Sufficient memory

A minimum of 64Kb is recommended for low-end use (such as storing names, telephone numbers and short memos). If you can, buy a model with 128Kb or more, especially if you have a large collection of contact names and details.

Search functions

The unit should offer quick & easy search functions, initiated by pressing a single button. Be wary of others requiring long key sequences to perform searches.

Navigation features

The ability to use a "pen" (a plastic pointing device shaped like a pen) to select functions and menus from the screen is useful, and can reduce the number of keystrokes required to access functions.

Alternatively, look for units that have multi-directional keys for scrolling.

Additional features

Make sure you only pay for features you will use - be realistic, and don't be persuaded by a smooth sales pitch.

Worthwhile features include the ability to link the unit to a PC (allowing you to print data and make backups), paging and fax functions.

Battery life

Batteries should last at least one year with constant use. Models that allow batteries to be swapped easily, and report low battery problems (via on-screen warnings) are preferable.

Upgradeability

Choose an upgradeable model. Buy the basic model, and upgrade as you need (and can afford) additional features.

Basic Functions

Your personal organiser should offer the following basic functions:

Time and data management tools

These include telephone numbers, contact list, scheduler, memo and so on.

Expenses and outgoings tracker

This is a specialised calculator for maintaining expense accounts. You should be able to store both numerical data (the amount) and text (so that you can include a one or two word summary of the expense e.g. petrol).

Currency/unit conversion tool

Tools such as these can be handy, especially if you travel often or deal with clients overseas. Basically, these allow you to convert currency and measurements between different systems (such as £ to $US or centimetres to inches).

World calendar and time zones

Advanced personal organisers include a world map with time zones marked. Make sure this is updateable, so it can be changed to allow for daylight saving.

Password protection

If security is an issue, ensure that your personal organiser allows you to password protect your data.

Voice messages

Some newer personal organisers can be used to record brief messages.

This is handy to record reminders, telephone numbers and memos when you can't use the keyboard (for instance, if you are walking or driving).

Feature overkill

Some manufacturers of personal organisers promise the world: easy text input, powerful data manipulation, quick faxing and even Internet access. Investigate every claim, and determine all the costs involved.

Many units, for example, offer modem/fax capabilities - but the necessary hardware and software costs extra. Similarly, models that link up to a computer may need software which is not included in the purchase price. Have the salesperson demonstrate features that interest you.

Warranty

Choose a well-known brand, and ask about service, warranty and the availability of replacement parts before you buy.

An All-In-One Unit?

Keep an eye out for a new breed of personal organisers, which integrate mobile phone technology.

Flip the unit on one side to make mobile phone calls. Turn it over to access your data!

The recently released Nokia 9000 Communicator (featured in the movie *The Saint*), is taking the industry by storm.

These models are "leading edge" technology, and have a price tag to suit. However, if you are also planning to buy a mobile phone, an all-in-one unit may prove less costly and more useful than buying each one separately.

Chapter 11

Buying an Office PC

Buying a computer is hard work! Technology changes rapidly; new gadgets become available, "old" gadgets become extinct - keeping track of it all is not easy!

My first PC, which I bought 10 years ago, was an IBM-compatible XT. It cost around £1200, and had 640Kb of RAM, a 40Mb hard disk drive, a 360Kb 5.25-inch floppy disk drive, and a CGA monitor. (If this doesn't make a lot of sense to you, don't despair. The technology guide in this chapter will help you get up to speed with the basics.)

For under £1000 today you can pick up a Pentium 200Mhz PC with around 4Gb of hard disk space, a massive 32Mb of RAM, a Super VGA colour monitor and lots of software bundled in the package!!!

Buying the right computer for your office is not easy. Choose carefully - as this can mean the difference between owning a productivity tool and a productivity drain.

CPU Speed

If you plan to use your computer for only the simplest tasks, a 486-based PC may suffice (you should be able to pick one up second-hand). In most cases, however, a Pentium-based PC is the better choice.

In the Pentium range, don't buy anything slower than a 166Mhz PC. Pentium CPUs slower than this will soon have difficulty running standard office software!

RAM

The cost of RAM has dropped significantly in the last 12 months. Take advantage of this by buying at least 16Mb - 32Mb if you run large database, graphics or multimedia programs. If you run several programs at once, buy 64Mb of RAM - especially if you plan to use Windows 95 (or Windows 98) or Windows NT.

TIP

Check a PC magazine for up-to-date prices, and information on the latest technology.

There is small price difference, but improvements in performance are astounding.

Hard disk capacity

The cost of hard disks has also decreased dramatically in recent years. An average hard disk now costs less than 25p per megabyte of disk space, compared with several pounds per megabyte a few years ago.

The smallest hard disks available can store 1Gb of data, and this will suit most small or home businesses. However, it is wise to plan ahead, so buy at least 2Gb of hard disk space if you can afford it.

Again, you will find that the price difference is small compared to the additional amount of space.

Video adapter

There is little to distinguish the various brands of video adapters. Most come with 1Mb of video RAM, which is sufficient for basic office use.

If you plan to use your PC for advanced tasks - such as graphics manipulation, multimedia or presentations - buy a video adapter with 2Mb or even 4Mb of video RAM. There is a difference between some of these more expensive cards, so shop around to ensure you get value for money.

Monitor

Computer monitors are one of the few items of hardware that have not fallen in price in recent times. In fact, they are now among the most expensive components, with basic 14-inch monitors costing around £120.

Most desktop systems are supplied with a 14-inch monitor. These are fine for day-to-day office use. However, if you use your PC extensively, consider spending an extra £75 or so on a 15-inch monitor - the extra inch really does make a world of difference, and is far gentler on the eyes.

If you plan to do serious graphics or CAD (computer aided drafting) work, a 17-inch monitor is a wise investment. However, these can easily add £350 or more to the cost of your computer.

TECHNICAL TIPS

RAM = Random Access Memory

A RAM module is an electrical device used by computers to temporarily store information (such as the text on your computer screen) before it is either discarded or saved to disk. Most people describe RAM in terms of thinking space – the more RAM your computer has, the more information that it can manipulate at any one time.

Video Adapter

A Video Adapter is the piece of hardware used by a PC to display text and images on the monitor. A video adapter uses its own memory (RAM) for storing video display information, so that the main RAM is not wasted.

PCMCIA Card

PCMCIA (Personal Computer Memory Card International Association) cards are also known as PC Cards, and are used for adding additional components and functions to notebook computers. Many notebooks accessories, such as modems, are bought in the form of PCMCIA cards.

Modem

A modem is a device that allows a computer to transmit data and other information over telephone lines.

CD-ROM = Compact Disk Read Only Memory

The CD-ROM drives used in computers are similar to stereo CD players, in that they read information stored permanently on a compact disk. CD-ROM drives are generally rated according to how fast they can read information from a CD. The original CD-ROM drives were referred to as "single speed". The next generation were "double speed", as they were roughly twice as fast as the earlier model. Today we have CD-ROM drives which operate at up to 24 times the speed of the first generation CD-ROM drives.

Soundcard

A computer which has a sound card fitted can output near-stereo quality sound and music from external speakers, as well as accept and record sound input using a microphone.

UPS = Uninterruptible Power Supply

A power supply that both filters and blocks harmful power spikes and surges (thereby protecting the PC from damage) as well as providing battery backup which will supply up to 15 minutes of power in the event of a blackout.

CPU = Central Processing Unit

The CPU is the "heart and soul" of the computer. It is responsible for the millions of computations that the computer performs each second — whether doing spreadsheet calculations or simply wordprocessing. A computer is usually classified by the speed of its CPU; for example, Pentium-based computers use Pentium-classed CPUs, 486 computers use the 80486 CPUs.

Accessories
Modem

Modems have several uses within the electronic or small business office. Primarily, they allow your computer to connect to other computers and exchange files and information.

If you telecommute, your modem is used to remotely access your employer's computer network, so that you can use your home computer to work on files stored on computers at head office.

If you work for yourself, you might choose to use a desktop PC at your office, and a notebook when you are on the road. With the right equipment, you can connect your notebook to your office computer via your modem and access your files.

Most modems today also offer fax features; this means that you can use the modem (together with your computer) to send and receive faxes.

In addition to convenience, this offers potential savings on fax paper. You can fax a document directly from your wordprocessor, without printing it first. Similarly, incoming faxes can be viewed on screen, allowing you to decide whether they are worth printing.

If you wish to access the Internet, you will also need a modem. (We take a closer look at how you can use the Internet in your business in Chapter 13.)

In short, no office, large or small, should be without a fax modem.

The electronic secretary

Voice-capable fax modems, which have only recently become affordable, are proving to be the electronic equivalent of a secretary - just what every electronic office needs!

These modems are essentially a hybrid of a standard fax modem and a soundcard. As such, a voice-modem can double as a sophisticated answering machine.

Voice-modems can detect if an incoming call is from another modem, a fax machine or a standard telephone, and react accordingly.

> **TIP**
>
> *Monitor size is measured from one corner at the base of the screen to the corner diagonally opposite. There is, however, no industry standard on how these measurements are taken. It comes as no surprise, then, that some 14-inch monitors actually have more viewing area than a few 15-inch models. The moral? Make sure that you get what you pay for!*

An incoming fax will be directed to the fax modem, which will collect the facsimile. A data call will be accepted by the modem, which will connect to the other computer. An incoming telephone call will be passed on to your normal telephone and, if it is not answered after a set number of rings, will be answered by the modem with your recorded message, and the caller's message will be recorded.

More advanced models can transfer calls, or call you at a specified number (such as a different office or your mobile) to play back recorded messages over the phone.

Most voice-capable modems contain audio chips, and do not require a sound card for basic options, such as playing recorded messages. However, if your PC does have a sound card, sound quality will be superior.

Modem Buyer's Guide
BT approval

Before a modem can be connected to a telephone line, it must first obtain BT approval. Look for the BT approval sticker. If in doubt, ask the dealer. Do not buy a non-BT approved modem.

Speed of *at least* 28.8kbps

The bps rating indicates how much information the modem can send or receive per second ("bps" = bits-per-second).

Until recently, 28.8kbps was the industry standard for affordable modems. However, there are now faster, but still affordable, modems on the market: the 36.6kbps and 56kbps models. If you can afford it, buy the fastest modem available as it will increase the amount of data you can send and receive.

Software

Make sure your modem comes with associated modem software. Many modems on the market today come bundled with Internet software preconfigured to access a particular (or a number of) ISPs. Ordinary communications software, which you can use to connect to any number of Bulletin Board Services in your area, is also usually included.

If you buy a fax modem, make sure it comes with software that allows you to send and receive faxes. More importantly, make sure the software isn't "crippled" - that is, that you can only use it a limited number of times before having to buy another, more expensive, software product.

Cables

Make sure your external modem comes with the cables necessary to connect it to your computer and the telephone jack, and that it includes a power supply (if one is required).

Multimedia

There are several good reasons to purchase a PC with multimedia capabilities.

Multimedia training and resources

Many business-related multimedia titles are available on CD-ROM, such as training courses, information databases, telephone directories and business guides. These can be a boon for the home office, providing easy access to sophisticated information and training resources.

CD-only software packages

Many office software packages occupy more than 100Mb of hard disk space, and use over 20 installation disks. It only takes one corrupt or missing disk to cause chaos, especially if you are re-installing software.

CD-ROMs, on the other hand, are less likely to suffer media defects. In addition, they streamline installation, and make storage easier.

Increasingly, software is being distributed on CD-ROM - and eventually you may not be able to get software on floppy disks.

Microsoft and other software houses have already started to discontinue floppy disk-based versions of many of their products, preferring instead to ship CD-ROM versions, which are cheaper to package and produce.

In addition, many software publishers place additional software (such as video-based tutorials and free third party software) on the CD-ROM versions, which are not available on disk-based versions.

Save hard disk space

Many software packages are now designed to run completely from CD-ROM, with the result that you do not have to sacrifice valuable hard disk space to access the package.

Choosing a CD-ROM Drive

Unless you are especially impatient and count every millisecond, there is little to distinguish between the basic functions of multimedia kits on the market. However, these tips can help when choosing a CD-ROM drive:

Name brands

Well-known name brands, such as Panasonic, Creative and Sony are preferable to unfamiliar brands.

Speed

Standard CD-ROMs are 16-speed, but 24-speed units are available (there are even faster units poised to enter the market).

However, before automatically buying the latest technology, decide whether you really need the extra speed. If not, you might save a few hundred dollars.

Bundles

Don't be fooled by a "bundle". Many multimedia kits include free CD titles to entice you to buy. However, you may not have much use for the "bonus" software.

If you can, choose applications that will be useful in your day-to-day business activities, rather than game-pack bundles. Be sure to check the quality of the hardware before being persuaded by the software.

Reviews

Read reviews in PC magazines which rate brands that offer the best value and price. Multimedia prices can fluctuate between retailers, so it pays to shop around.

Buy with the PC

Buy multimedia with the PC rather than as an upgrade. You can save (on labour costs at least) if you buy the hardware with a complete system.

Choosing a sound card

Your sound card is an important part of your multimedia kit. However, unless you plan to use your system for specialist audio applications, there is little difference between basic sound cards. All will play music from your audio CDs, as well as sound effects from your favourite game, and audio commentary from your video-learning CD-ROM.

Most multimedia kits are bundled, and you cannot mix and match hardware. To avoid potential conflicts with your multimedia software, stick to well-known sound-card brands.

Around The Corner

CD-ROM technology on the horizon promises to reform the current multimedia marketplace.

The Digital Video Disk (also known as a Digital Versatile Disk or DVD) offers a storage capacity of 4.7Gb, compared to the standard CD capacity of 600Mb.

This means titles that currently span several CDs will fit onto a single DVD-ROM. It also makes it possible to squeeze a full-length motion picture onto a single CD for digital playback!

A single DVD-ROM can store and play back up to two hours of full-motion movie, video, and audio on either your PC or your TV. As such, they may soon rival the VCR!

This new hardware will be backward compatible; that is, it will be able to play the older (current) CD-ROMs and audio CDs, so you will not lose your investment in CDs. It is unlikely, however, that the DVD technology will work on current CD-ROM drives.

What To Look For

The basic specifications for a typical home-office needs are as follows:

- Pentium 166Mhz CPU.
- 256K cache.
- 16Mb RAM (32Mb preferred).
- 1.44Mb floppy (standard on all models).
- 1Gb hard disk drive (2Gb preferred).
- 1Mb video adaptor (2Mb or more for serious graphics work).
- 14-inch SVGA non-interlaced monitor (15-inch digital SVGA monitor preferred).
- Desktop or mini-tower case with 200W power supply.
- 104-key enhanced keyboard.
- Two- or three-button mouse.
- Mousepad.

TIP

Microsoft's Office 97 Professional software package needs almost 200Mb of hard disk space for complete installation. Other office packages require similar amounts — making it easy to see why an 1Gb hard disk drive is an absolute minimum!

Chapter 12

Buying a Printer

Your printer - or more accurately, the quality of its output - can tell your clients a lot about your company. Printing which looks unprofessional can scare off potential clients, who will wonder about the quality of your other work.

A quality printer is therefore a good investment.

Two Types Of Printer

Business users can choose between ink jet or bubble jet printers (hereafter collectively referred to as "ink jet printers") and laser printers.

Dot matrix printers, although readily available and cheap, have no place in a professional office. One exception might be in accounting - dot matrix computers are traditionally used for printing internal accounting reports, point-of-sale receipts and invoices.

Ink jet printers

In the past, laser printers were the only serious choice for clear, crisp text. Ink jet printers tended to "smudge" their output and were only used for in-house documents, drafts and student assignments.

However, ink jet technology has advanced dramatically, and now offers quiet, quality printing with reasonable resolution (measured in dots-per-inch or "dpi").

Most ink jet printers offer a draft or economy mode as well as a standard printing mode. Do not buy an ink jet printer with less than a 300dpi standard printing rating. If you use your printer for graphics or presentations, choose a printer which can output at 600dpi.

In short, today's ink jet printers are an economical option for most businesses, and offer near-laser quality.

Laser printers

Laser printers offer professional quality printing. Output starts at 600dpi (with 300dpi for drafts), increasing to 800 and 1200dpi. Output from printers at 1200dpi or better is considered typeset quality (on a par with magazines and books).

Laser printers produce good results, but have a price tag to match. For instance, a laser printer that can output text and graphics at 600 to 800dpi costs about £300.

However, there are a number of relatively inexpensive laser printers on the market, specifically designed with the small business in mind. Your computer dealer should be able to advise you of these products and their advantages.

Printer Features

When buying a printer, you need to consider four major issues: print quality, print speed, internal memory size and print cycle rating.

Print speed

An average printer processes between six and 10 pages per minute ("ppm"). This is quite satisfactory for most SOHOs.

However, if you find productivity suffers as a result of waiting for printed output, you may need to buy another printer, or one with a faster output.

High-end printers can print upwards of 12 pages per minute. However, this additional speed is costly.

Internal memory

Most printers have internal memory installed, where data for the current print job is stored. This speeds up printing, which is faster when data is stored in the printer's memory rather than sent from the PC a section at a time.

Most printers have 1Mb to 2Mb of internal memory, which is generally sufficient for small offices.

However, if you intend using your printer for large documents and heavy graphics, or if several users will be sharing a printer, investigate printers with 4Mb or 6Mb of built-in RAM (most internal memories are upgradeable).

Print cycle rating

Printers are rated according to the number of pages they can comfortably print per month.

Although high-end printers can print over 20,000 pages per month, the average SOHO is unlikely to exceed a thousand or so a month. As a general rule, the higher the print cycle rating of a particular printer, the higher its cost.

Costs

Everyone knows that purchase price is only one aspect of the overall cost of car ownership. Registration and licensing fees, petrol, oil and maintenance costs can contribute substantially to the overall cost.

Similarly, computers and peripherals have hidden costs. Running costs over the lifetime of a specific computer or peripheral often far outweigh its initial purchase cost. For this reason, it can be more economical to buy an expensive printer that requires less service and maintenance than to buy a cheap one.

The facts

Ink jets generally cost less than half the price of a comparable laser printer. However, these savings can be cancelled out by running costs.

Firstly, ink jet cartridges cost more per page of output than laser toner cartridges. If you print several hundred pages per month, this can add up. On the other hand, if you only expect to print a hundred pages or so a month (including correspondence, invoices and internal documents), ink jets can be economical.

Ink jet "friendly" paper, which enhances print quality by reducing smudging and bleeding, also costs significantly more than standard laser paper.

Finally, the cost of replacement printer cartridges needs to be investigated. Some cartridges can be re-inked or recycled, reducing costs significantly.

Choosing a printer

Use this checklist when deciding which printer is best for you:

❑   How many pages will I print each month?

Most printers stipulate a print cycle rating, as discussed above. If you intend printing more than a few thousand pages a month, investigate "industrial strength" printers, which can print large numbers of pages economically.

☐ What quality output do I need?

This is central when choosing between a laser and ink jet printer.

Do your print your own tender documents or marketing brochures? If so, the high quality a laser printer offers is essential. If you outsource your special printing requirements, an ink jet should suffice.

TIP

Some printer manufacturers earn a larger margin on printer cartridges than on the actual printer! They reason that selling as many printers as possible (even at a lower than usual profit margin) boosts their user base of the replacement printer cartridges. By selling these at a mark-up, they cannot lose, as they have a captive market — either you buy new printer cartridges, or your printer is worthless. The moral of the story? Check out the cost of replacement cartridges before you buy.

☐ Will I frequently print graphics, or is my output usually plain text?

Some printers (especially those with less internal memory) find printing graphics hard going and others cannot produce quality graphic output. Be sure to put any proposed printer through its paces, including "real life" printing examples.

☐ Do I want to print in colour?

Most ink jet printers will print in either colour or black ink (depending on which cartridge you install). But there are differences in print quality among the various "colour" ink jet printers. Beware of impressive-looking demonstration prints that use expensive colour printing paper, as they will not achieve the same quality on normal paper.

☐ Do I need access to a wide range of fonts? (Fonts are different styles of typeface characters.)

☐ Do I require two or more paper trays?

If you use pre-printed paper (such as paper with a letterhead), a second tray can save time and effort, allowing you to print letters using both letterhead and plain paper without reloading. However, if you use wordprocessing software which prints letterheads at the same time as text, you are unlikely to need a second tray.

☐ Do I want to print on different size paper?

Most printers can handle A4 and US letter-size paper. If you want to use paper of any other size you will need to look for a specialist printer. For instance, few printers will handle A3-size paper. Others experience problems printing on thick paper or transparencies.

Be sure that the printer you select can handle the types and sizes of paper you want to work with.

Shopping Around

Be aware that printer pricing varies from store to store, and it is wise to shop around. You can save even more if you buy your printer at the same time as your PC. Many stores will sell a printer at cost (often up to a hundred pounds less than the recommended price) in order to clinch a PC sale.

New Developments

Windows-only printers (both laser and ink jet) are now available, at a price significantly lower than that of their standard counterparts.

Often known as "GDI printers", these rely on the Windows operating system and your computer hardware to perform many of the standard printer functions, such as spooling information, preparing graphics for printing, and sending information to the printer. As a result, the printer hardware is minimal, and the printers are compact in size.

There are a few downsides to GDI printers. They tend to work erratically with DOS-based programs, and are often slower than standard printers (especially if your PC is busy with other tasks at the time of printing).

But, on the whole, the quality of these printers is satisfactory, and you certainly cannot complain about the price.

Chapter 13

Buying a Scanner

For many years, scanners have been the elitist tool of desktop publishers and computer enthusiasts. Now, however, quality scanners are within the reach of home and home-office users.

Early scanners were pen-like, capable of scanning printed text one line at a time. The accuracy of these scanners was dubious, even when used in perfect conditions.

"Hand-held" scanners followed. These had a larger scanning area and involved dragging the device across the text or graphics. Quality scans required the scanner to be dragged in a straight line, which often made scanning books or folded materials impossible.

More recently flatbed scanners, which look and operate like photocopiers, have been released. Flatbed scanners are now quite affordable, and provide excellent quality scans.

Why Buy a Scanner?

You may find a scanner useful for any - or all - of the tasks below.

Digitise records for storage

Scan in copies of invoices, receipts, correspondence and similar paper-based records, and save them to disk, CD-ROM or backup tape, in case something should happen to the original.

A single backup tape or CD-ROM containing scanned images of thousands of paper records occupies considerably less space than the originals.

The paperless office

Although we have long been promised the paperless office, it is still far from a reality. Businesses receive large quantities of printed material, in the form of correspondence, magazines, reports and so on. Rather than storing this non-essential information in folders or filing cabinets, why not scan it and save the digital files on disk?

Create your own electronic library

Documents that have been scanned into your computer are in digital format, and can therefore be passed on to friends and colleagues on disk or via electronic mail. They can also be filed on your computer, or indexed using special software, which will allow you to search them using keywords.

Generate images

If you publish your own marketing literature or a regular newsletter, you can use your scanner to create custom images of products, or snippets from other printed media. Similarly, if you plan to establish a Web site, a scanner makes creating your own online brochures and catalogues much easier.

Optical Character Recognition

Perhaps one of the most valuable uses of scanners is OCR - optical character recognition. Using OCR technology, paper documents can be scanned and converted to electronic text more cheaply and with less fuss than typing them in or hiring a data entry company.

Once in electronic format, the text can be imported into wordprocessing documents (such as newsletters or reports) or into a central database or spreadsheet.

OCR technology allows the conversion of static documents into accessible electronic text, which can be easily copied, distributed, indexed and searched.

Choosing a Scanner

Although less expensive, hand-held scanners do not offer the same quality as flatbed scanners, as they are susceptible to "hand shake" - if you do not hold your hand steady during the scanning process, it can distort the image. This can be near impossible when scanning an entire page of text. For these reasons, a hand-held scanner is not a good choice for your office.

Colour or greyscale

The first decision is whether to buy a colour or greyscale scanner. Colour scanners are more expensive than greyscale models (though only just).

Determine what you will use the scanner for. If you only want to scan written material, a colour scanner will be superfluous. On the other hand, a colour scanner is necessary to scan photos and other images in colour.

If in doubt, choose a colour model. Although you might not be able to think of any benefits of colour over black-and- white scanning at first, in time you will!

Sheetfed or flatbed scanners

A sheetfed scanner draws the page to be scanned across the scanning window, much like a facsimile machine draws in the document to be faxed. Sheetfed scanners are smaller and cheaper than flatbed scanners. However, they can be impractical if you need to scan text from a book or magazine, as these cannot be fed through the scanner (the pages need to be photocopied first, which may affect the image quality).

Choose the scanner which best suits your needs. If you only need to scan an occasional piece of correspondence or photocopied article, a sheetfed scanner will be fine. Otherwise, you are better off purchasing a flatbed.

Resolution

The higher the dpi rating of a scanner, the better the scan quality. The minimum requirement for professional looking scans is 300 dpi - 600 dpi is preferable.

Many scanners make use of interpolation technology, which allows them to achieve a higher dpi - often more than 1200 dpi. Although these scanners cost more, the quality of their output is worth the investment.

Be sure to ask for a demonstration of the scanner and its output, preferably scanning images or text similar to that which you are likely to process.

It's all in the bundle

A scanner is useless without software to capture and manipulate the scanned image or text. Most scanners are bundled with all the software necessary to get you started.

Often, however, it is the software rather than the hardware that determines the quality of the scan. Poor integration between the bundled software and the scanner can make scanning a nightmare. When choosing a scanner, do your homework, and keep an eye out for software packages which have been favourably reviewed in PC magazines and other publications.

Chapter 14

Harnessing the Internet

The Internet offers businesses in the 90s so many challenges that, not surprisingly, managers and executives often feel overwhelmed and confused both by the technology and the opportunities and risks it presents.

A number of smaller businesses feel that the established, larger corporations have most to gain from the Internet, as they can afford to invest in new technology, training and consultants to help management face those challenges.

But it is the smaller, newer companies that are currently embracing the Internet, eager to harness its power and its profit-enhancing potential.

Smaller But Nimble

Small businesses occasionally find themselves "out resourced" by their bigger competitors, who have more staff, larger marketing budgets and better trained executives and salespeople.

As a small business owner, it is important to realise your size gives you an important edge, especially in terms of flexibility and responsiveness to customer and market needs.

To harness these advantages, your office needs to operate at peak efficiency, especially if you are a sole proprietor. To achieve this you should maximise your technology investment. Perhaps the most rewarding investment you can make is to connect to the Internet.

What is the Internet?

The Internet is a computer network that connects nearly all countries and is used by 30 to 50 million people. The sheer size of this online community, and the fact that it touches every corner of the earth, makes the Internet both a revolutionary social and business tool.

Advantages For Small Business

Even in its developmental years, many predicted the Internet would be a boon for small businesses since it offers the first true level-playing field.

There are few barriers to entering the online market. The cost of an Internet connection is minimal, and the tools and hardware needed to use it effectively are within the means of most small businesses.

On the Internet small companies can compete side-by-side with larger ones. All have access to tools such as email and Web sites, which appear the same whether they originate from an expensive office network or a stand-alone PC.

Similarly, there is no online equivalent to the CBD - it is irrelevant to those who visit your Web site whether it is hosted by a premium or a budget Internet Service Provider (ISP).

The effectiveness of your Internet presence depends on how you implement it. The small or home office is at no real disadvantage compared to its larger competitors. If anything, large companies are disadvantaged, due to the delays they often experience in making and implementing decisions.

Email

Email is correspondence sent electronically from computer to computer over a network. Email is one of the most important business tools provided by the Internet, and offers a fast, cheap means of communication.

For instance, you might want the latest price list from an international supplier. You can ask to have it faxed to you, assuming it is in faxable form (a booklet, for instance, would first have to be photocopied). If the price list is large, your supplier might prefer to send it by mail or overnight courier.

In each case the price list arrives in static form. If you wish to use the new prices in a database or spreadsheet, you will have to enter them manually and then check the entries for accuracy.

Email is far more flexible. Simply phone your supplier and ask for the price list to be emailed. Your supplier connects to the Internet, composes an email message addressed to you, attaches a copy of the computer file containing the price list, and sends it.

Within seconds you will receive the email and can view the price list on your computer.

If you wish, you can print a copy or transfer information from the price list into your spreadsheet or database. Either way, you have the information within seconds, and you have received it in a far more useable form!

Reach Out and Email Someone

Email can also be used to stay in touch with customers. Pretty well anything you might print or fax to a client, such as quotations, reports, or project proposals, can be sent by email.

Using email not only saves you the cost of printing and mailing, but the client receives the information faster, and can respond to it immediately (such as accepting your quote or requesting further information).

Many clients find communicating by email more convenient than more traditional forms of business communications. Email can be sent after business hours and is cheap, even if the recipient is on the other side of the world.

Electronic mail, then, provides businesses with almost instantaneous communications as well as an opportunity to reduce office overheads.

The World Wide Web

Thanks to the Web, anyone with access to the Internet can publish information online quickly and easily, making it accessible to millions of Internet users.

Already the Web is being used to distribute electronic books, newspapers and magazines, government reports, court decisions and much more. People are using the Web to self-publish poems and books, and to air their views on many topics.

The Web has transformed the Internet from a dreary, text-based interface into a point-and-click graphical environment bursting with sound, colour, animation and video - a truly multimedia medium.

Businesses have harnessed the Internet's user-friendly qualities and multimedia functions to develop online "shopfronts". Visitors to these Web sites can view images (even video) and descriptions of products and services the business offers. Vendors and consumers can interact, allowing the former to respond to individual customers' needs and solicit feedback and comments.

The Web and Small Business

Online, small businesses can compete on an even keel with larger competitors in developing and implementing successful Internet strategies.

Smaller businesses have the advantage of being able to start small, think fast and implement their vision quickly. Although many large corporations realise the importance of the Web, red tape and office politics can - and often does - prevent them from establishing an online presence.

Of course, few people get their Web sites right immediately. To be an effective sales tool, a Web site must be monitored and refined in response to customer feedback.

Getting Connected

All you need to obtain an Internet connection is a relatively modern computer, a modem and a telephone line.

Your Internet Service Provider will generally supply you with the software you need to connect, including email and a Web browser. Once online, you can download additional free or demonstration software.

The cost of a standard, dial-up Internet connection is quite low. Competition has forced costs down over the last few years, with regular users now paying as little as £50 per year for unlimited use. Considering that this enables you to explore Net sites around the world - not to mention communicating with others both nationally and internationally - this is remarkably cheap.

Of course, there are more expensive access options, such as ISDN (which is much faster) or even a permanent Internet connection for those who rely heavily on email for business communications.

To learn more about specific aspects of the Internet, look out for other books from Net.Works:

The Complete Beginner's Guide to the Internet will teach you more about the basics of the Internet, such as how to get connected, what resources it offers and how to access them.

The Complete Beginner's Guide to the World Wide Web focuses on the most popular section of the Net where most information and businesses are based.

Entrepreneurs will find *The Experts Business Guide to the Internet* useful, as it explains how to use the Net to increase profits. (For more information and an order form see Pages 94-95).

Benefits Of An Internet Connection

Business-to-business

Streamline your communications with suppliers, distributors and other business contacts.

Businesses are increasingly using the Internet to stay in touch, using the cheap and efficient facilities offered by email.

Business-to-consumers

The Internet can enhance your communications with clients, offering faster responses to queries and orders than is possible by telephone and mail.

The Internet provides consumers with access to both Web sites (for general information) and email (which allows customers to ask for more specific or personalised information).

Colleague-to-colleague

The Internet hosts a number of discussion forums that staff can use to meet and keep in touch with other industry members. These are useful for keeping an eye on industry trends, discussing government and other policy agendas, and establishing useful contacts.

Chapter 15

Difficulties Facing the Mobile Office

Setting up a mobile office sounds simple. The combination of a mobile phone and a notebook computer will enable you to conduct business anywhere, any time - or will it?

Unfortunately, using your computer and other business tools on the move can make you feel that you are caught in the middle of a pitched battle.

Mobile phone "drop outs", lack of or a poor signal and flat batteries (both phone and computer) are familiar problems. But the mobile office can set many more hurdles in your way.

This chapter examines some of the practical difficulties of using your new equipment while on the move.

A Really Mobile Telephone

Choosing the right mobile phone is important. In addition to deciding on a telephone service provider and tariff plan, the model purchased plays an important role.

A mobile phone with a good antenna and long battery life, and a service provider that offers good, UK-wide coverage (both in rural and urban areas) are essential. Finding yourself on the road with a dead battery or no signal can bring your productivity to a halt.

If you travel by car, choose a battery charger with an adapter that allows it to plug into the car's cigarette lighter (as well as standard power sockets). A battery charger with a "rapid charge" option is useful to minimise your total downtime, although these can be costly.

International Roaming

If your work takes you abroad, you need to be sure of three things: that your mobile phone is a digital (GSM) phone; that it has "roaming" capabilities; and that your telephone service provider has roaming agreements with providers in the country you are visiting.

When you buy your mobile phone and subscribe to a telephone service provider, a small "smart card" is inserted into the phone. This contains all the information the phone needs to operate within the service provider's mobile phone network. Regardless of where you go in Britain, it will be able to locate the nearest base station.

However, when you travel overseas, your mobile phone cannot operate because it is not able to locate a nearby base station; that is, not unless it can roam. When your mobile phone is in roaming mode, it connects to a local telephone service provider affiliated with your provider, and uses its mobile network to make and receive calls.

Calls made (and sometimes those received) while roaming overseas will cost more. Ask your telephone service provider for full details of costs.

Modem Jack Problems

Using a notebook and modem on the road can create many problems. For instance, the motel or hotel you are staying at may not have a modem-friendly jack to plug your modem into.

Even if you can plug your modem in, you might have difficulties getting a dial tone. Most motels and hotels use PABX telephone systems, which allow guests to use one-digit numbers for service calls.

PABX systems are well known for the problems they can cause modems. However, you can get around this. Read the handbook in the room that explains how to make outside telephone calls. Normally this involves dialling "0" or "1" before the telephone number. If this is the case, you will need to manually edit the dialling dialogue box of your fax or Internet software to insert the required digit. Be sure to insert a comma between the required digit and the number to be called. The comma instructs your modem to wait a second after dialling the digit to give the PABX system enough time to supply a dial tone.

For example, to call 0123 2345, edit the number to read: 0,0123 2345

However, some hotels and motels do not have telephone sockets in the rooms, as the phones are wired directly to the wall. In short, it pays to find out whether a hotel or motel is "modem friendly" before you book.

TIP

An obvious solution to the modem and wall socket quandary is to buy a mobile phone that can be used with a modem. This way you can use your modem wherever you are.

Also, be wary of the price of your modem calls from the hotel room. Some hotels charge exhorbitant rates for STD calls, and a few even charge for local calls on a timed basis.

Power Adapters

You will not always have access to a power socket, so be sure to buy an adapter that allows you to plug your notebook or mobile phone charger into a car's cigarette lighter. Alternatively, purchase spare batteries, and re-charge these wherever possible.

If you travel overseas, you may find that your power adapters do not fit the power socket used in another country. Alternatively, the power source might not be compatible with your equipment. It is wise to investigate these issues before departure.

There are now a number of "international traveller" kits on the market that contain all the power adapters and conditioners needed for the country you are visiting. Although these kits can cost up to £50, the peace of mind they offer is worth that.

Power Regulators

Not all countries have a reliable power supply. Some have regular power fluctuations and spikes. These can damage sensitive electronic equipment, such as your modem or notebook. Be sure to invest in a power regulator suitable for the country that you are visiting. These can be purchased from most electronics shops.

Chapter 16

Time Management

Many people start their own business to reclaim quality time. Tired of working for a boss, they also look forward to the added security and independence self-employment brings.

While little compares to the thrill of your first "self-earned" pay cheque, and the sense of responsibility that comes with running your own business, you may not find that time stretches to meet your needs.

The reality is that self-employment often spills over into that elusive quality time. Late nights, early starts and the occasional financial concern can spread a dark cloud over your recreational and family time.

Unless you actively maintain a separate work and home life, you may discover that the sought after quality time never arrives.

Time Management

The complaint heard most often from clients and business colleagues is that there are simply not enough hours in a day. Time is a valuable commodity, and those who can use it efficiently are at an advantage.

Complete this self-test to determine how you use your time:

Carry a small notebook or diary with you. Each day, record when you wake, when you start and finish work, and each activity you undertake in between. Note everything you do, no matter how routine or trifling.

At the end of the week, tally the number of hours you have spent working. From that number, subtract the following:

☐   Time spent talking socially on the telephone.

☐   Time wasted looking for misplaced files, documents and so on.

☐   Time wasted waiting on hold for clients and services.

☐ Time wasted in between activities.

☐ Time spent on lunch, coffee and snack breaks.

☐ Time wasted during working hours listening to the radio, watching TV, reading magazines and so on.

☐ Time spent travelling to visit clients or run errands.

You'll probably be surprised at the amount of time you waste each day on unnecessary, unproductive tasks.

Your immediate priority should be to halve this wasted time. In the long term, aim to eliminate all time-wasting activities.

Planning

Lack of daily planning can waste time. How often do you make a trip to purchase goods or visit clients, only to zigzag back and forth across town? How often have you repeated or aborted trips because you had forgotten something? All of these time wasters can be avoided if you plan your day effectively.

Procrastination

Do you have files full of unfinished tasks, which have been put on hold while you attend to something "more important"?

It takes time to focus on a task, and interruptions can make it necessary to refocus each time you re-attempt a task. Procrastination can be a serious drain on productivity.

Make a List

Have you ever concluded a conversation with a client (in person or over the telephone) and then realised that you have not discussed all the issues you needed to?

Calling or visiting the client again can be costly (and look unprofessional) and is a time waster. Before making calls or visits, consider the issues you need to cover, and make a list to guide your conversation.

Communicate with clients and colleagues in the most suitable and time-efficient manner. For instance, a query which requires an immediate response can be best handled on the telephone, while other queries can be sent by email or fax.

If a client is unavailable, but has a secretary or voicemail service, take advantage of this fact and leave a detailed message, indicating the precise reason(s) for your call, so that the client can be prepared when s/he calls back.

Paper Shuffle

It is almost impossible to avoid paperwork in business. Most is self-generated, but some is received from third parties. Be strict when deciding what paperwork to keep or follow up. If a letter or brochure is not immediately useful, throw it away or file it in a "follow-up" folder (and be sure to follow it up!). Keep the paperwork around your office to a minimum.

Meetings

Meetings are the scourge of the 1990s. It seems that everyone needs to meet before making a decision. If workers spent as much time being productive as they spend in meetings discussing how to be productive, time management would no longer be an issue!

Meetings are useful if you cannot communicate with clients efficiently by telephone or in writing.

Only call a meeting once you have a detailed itinerary of issues to discuss, and ensure that the participants are familiar with this itinerary before meeting.

During a meeting you should take every step possible to conclude or otherwise deal with the issues set on the itinerary (although this may be difficult if you are not chairing the meeting). Avoid leaving matters undecided - this will only result in further unproductive meetings.

Idle Time

Idle time is not necessarily wasted time. You may find yourself waiting for a response or input from a third party, but this does not mean that you should sit around twiddling your thumbs.

If it is inappropriate to hurry the third party along, use the spare time to prepare a checklist of jobs at hand. Return any outstanding telephone calls or reply to correspondence. Is there any outstanding filing? Could the office use a tidy?

Conclusion

Time management is about being aware of the value of your time, and refusing to allow others to waste it. Once you become aware of time-wasting activities or habits, and take steps to eradicate these, you will be surprised at just how much "extra" time you have.

Appendix

Your Business Plan

Developing a business plan involves detailed planning, and a frank and realistic analysis of your proposed business venture. Every aspect of your new business - from management and marketing to turnover, cashflow and profit expectations - should be detailed in writing.

Preparing a business plan will take time, and require honest research and assessment. At the end of the process you should have a good indication of the viability of your business.

Always remember that there are no "right" answers - a business plan is not a test. Don't "fudge" the numbers to make the venture look good on paper - you will not only be doing yourself (and any other potential investors) a disservice, but could also be setting yourself up for failure.

In this section we will look at the fundamentals of a business plan. While it is true that each company business plan is different, all follow the same "formula", and must, of necessity, include the same types of information.

If you have any concerns about the appropriateness of your business plans, or if you would like a "second opinion" of your financial estimates and other matters (always a good idea), consult your accountant or business advisor.

Developing a Business Plan

A business plan serves a number of purposes, but its primary use is to determine the nature and prospects of your company, and to convey the merits and disadvantages of the business to potential partners, investors or financiers.

Statement of purpose

Your business plan should begin with a statement of purpose.

State the nature of your business, how it will operate on a day-to-day basis and how you envisage it growing over both the short and long term. Include an analysis of the market (potential or actual) for your product or service, how much of that market you can expect to capture and how this will translate in financial terms.

Statement of business

Document how the business will be managed, the pivotal roles and responsibility of management, the businesses' primary function or role, and any secondary functions or roles.

Statement of business status

Describe the status of the business; that is, whether you are starting it from scratch, buying into an existing one or taking over a business.

If you are buying or taking over an existing business, detail its financial and trading history, as well as plans you have to alter it.

In this section you should also detail the legal structure of your business (for instance, if it is a company, include principal investors, directors and so on).

Statement of the market

Discuss in detail the market you want to target, including:

- Who your clients are.
- What products and/or services you will be selling.
- Why you feel there is a need for such services or products.
- Any characteristics of the market that may affect your business (positively or negatively).

Statement of competition

Set out in detail your competition in the marketplace (assuming it is an existing market). Include:

- Who your competitors are.
- How long your competitors have been in the market.
- Their strengths and weaknesses.
- The level of goodwill and loyalty they attract.

- How you will differentiate your products/services from theirs.

Statement of suppliers

State how reliant your business will be on suppliers of raw materials or services, the number and competitiveness of your suppliers, and the general terms upon which you will obtain your supplies.

Statement of finances

This is one of the most, if not the most, important sections of your business plan. You need to ensure that the details included are as accurate and realistic as possible.

State your personal investment in the company, whether you will need to draw a salary immediately, the current and potential cash flow of the business, realistic levels of profits that can be expected in both the short and long term, and whether the business has or requires loans or other debts.

This section should detail to the last pound the cost of "starting up" (that is, what you need to open your doors), including: legal and accounting costs (company incorporation and so on), marketing costs (brochures and so on), stationery, insurance, initial inventory, employee salaries and business equipment.

Also include proposed profit and loss statements based on a realistic and well-researched assessment of your likely income and overheads.

The Complete Beginner's Guide to The Internet

What exactly is The Internet? Where did it come from and where is it going? And, more importantly, how can everybody take their place in this new community?

The Complete Beginner's Guide to The Internet tells you:

- What types of resources are available for private, educational and business use,
- What software and hardware you need to access them,
- How to connect to and use The Internet via a modem or network,
- How you go about finding what you want,
- How to communicate with others, and
- The rules of the Superhighway, or 'netiquette'.

Price: £4.95

- ❑ Each reader will be eligible for 10 hours FREE Internet access, FREE Internet software and a FREE month's membership to CompuServe (a total package worth over £15).

The Complete Beginner's Guide to The World Wide Web

Scott Western, an acknowledged, British, World Wide Web expert, leads you through every aspect of THE WEB highlighting interesting sites, and showing you the best ways to find and retrieve the information you want. Discover:

- ✔ How to minimise your time on-line, saving you money
- ✔ Professional tricks for searching the Web
- ✔ How World Wide Web pages are designed and constructed
- ✔ All about domain names and getting your own web space **Price: £4.95**

Order Form

Please complete the form USING BLOCK CAPITALS and return to
TTL, PO Box 200, Harrogate HG1 2YR or fax to **01423-526035**

❑ I enclose a cheque/postal order for £_____ made payable to 'TTL'

❑ Please debit my Visa/ Mastercard/Amex Card No:

Book	Qty	Price

Postage: Over £8 FREE *Otherwise please add 50p per item within UK, £1.50 elsewhere*

Total:

Expiry date:

Signature:
Date:

Title: _____ Initials: _____
Name: _____
Address: _____
_____
_____ Postcode: _____
Daytime Telephone: _____

Please allow 14-21 days delivery.
We hope to make you further exciting offers in the future. If you do not wish to receive these, please write to us at the above address.

elecof

The Expert's Business Guide to The Internet

Also by Mark Neely

FREE UPDATES

Register, free of charge, to gain exclusive access to weekly on-line updates. All the latest news, plus columns on technologies and market strategies as well as links to hundreds of other Internet marketing and business-related sources.

You could say this book won't go out of date!!

Price: £24.95 including free updates

Order using the form opposite and claim a £5 discount =£19.95

The Internet is changing and evolving literally every day, each change bringing with it new opportunities and ideas for promotion and marketing. And this guide helps you explore all aspects of establishing yourself in this huge marketplace.

Written specifically for businesses wishing to establish a strong Internet presence, it takes you through the issues surrounding the development of electronic commerce (the digital economy) by explaining in **non-technical terms** what business on the Internet is all about.

The author closely examines the social dynamics and popular culture of the Net, which will play a large part in any strategy to commercially harness Cyberspace.

Also, in everyday language:

- What tools are available to help you incorporate the Net in your normal activities.
- What constitutes acceptable commercial activity on the Net - and what could cause your company to be 'flamed'.
- How to develop an integrated Internet strategy.
- How to ensure your business procedures compliment - not contradict - your Net activities.
- Privacy and Security when dealing with digital cash.

THE VERY BEST OF BUSINESS SHAREWARE!

For every FOUR you buy, you get ONE FREE

Here's your chance to acquire a great software library to evaluate FREELY in your home or office, on your own computer. All the programs listed on Pages 4 & 49 are Shareware, which means you and your family can evaluate them in your own time — and only pay a registration fee to the authors if and when you decide to use the program regularly. All have been specially selected from thousands of Shareware programs available.

Simply tick the box next to the disk or disks you wish to order, enclosing a postal order, cheque or credit card authorisation to the value of £2.75 per **1.44Mb high density 3.5- inch diskette** to cover the cost of the diskette, duplication, postage and handling. The ready reckoner in the order form makes it easy to calculate your cost.

REMEMBER: For every FOUR DISKS you order, select ONE DISK FREE!

PRIORITY ORDER FORM (photocopy acceptable)

TO: TTL, PO Box 200, Harrogate , N.Yorks HG1 2YR
(urgent credit card orders can be faxed to: 01423-526035)

please rush me the 3.5-inch windows shareware disks ticked below:

❑ EF-1   ❑ EF-2   ❑ EF-3   ❑ EF-4   ❑ EF-5

❑ EF-6   ❑ EF-7   ❑ EF-8   ❑ EF-9   ❑ EF-10

I enclose a postal order/cheque made out to 'TTL' to cover the cost of duplication, postage and handling for the amount in the box ticked below (calculated to give you every fifth disk free)

FREE DISKS

❑ 1 disk:£2.75   ❑ 2 disks:£5.50   ❑ 3 disks:£8.25   ❑ 4 disks:£11.00   ❑ 5 disks:£11.00

❑ 6 disks:£13.75   ❑ 7 disks:£16.50   ❑ 8 disks:£19.25   ❑ 9 disks:£22.00   ❑ 10 disks:£22.00

or charge my MasterCard/Visa/Amex no: _____   Expires: ___/___

Cardholder's signature: _____

Name: _____

Address: _____

_____

_____ P/Code _____   elecof